Easy Steps to Writing Fantastic Research Reports

BY MARIAM JEAN DREHER

KATHRYN A. DAVIS

PRISCILLA WAYNANT

SUZANNE F. CLEWELL

SCHOLASTIC
PROFESSIONAL BOOKS

NEW YORK • TORONTO • LONDON • AUCKLAND • SYDNEY
MEXICO CITY • NEW DELHI • HONG KONG

CREDITS

"Please Do My Homework," *Time*, January 23, 1995, p. 7.

Sally Forth © 1995 by Greg Howard. Reprinted with special permission of King Features Syndicate

Front cover design by Aartpack
Interior design by Kathy Massaro
Copyright © 2000 by Mariam Jean Dreher, Kathryn A. Davis, Priscilla Waynant, and Suzanne F. Clewell

ISBN: 0-590-97306-1
Printed in USA

Contents

A Research Model That Works

If you have picked up this book, you are probably concerned with some of the same things that led us to write it. We know that research projects have great potential for motivating students and helping them become independent learners. But we simply were not very happy with much of what we saw going on in our own and in others' classrooms when it came time for students to engage in research.

Why weren't we happy? A composite sketch of many different research projects we have observed helps to illustrate some of our reasons. Pretend you are working with intermediate-grade students when the time comes for them to use the classroom or library resources to find information on early settlers or state symbols or whales. Or perhaps it is time for them to write a report or create a poster or a multimedia presentation using the information they have found. As you observe the students, you will note that many of the lessons they have been taught seem to have been largely forgotten.

Alphabetical order, indexes, headings, types of resources, fragment notes, drafting, and revision—students seem to have little recall of lessons on such topics. You watch a "good" reader flip through a book on her topic, ignoring the table of contents and the index; she finally discards it because there is "nothing in it." You see another student waiting passively while the librarian finds the material for him. A long line forms at the CD encyclopedia even though most topics are better served by other sources. Another long line forms next to the teacher as the students line up to ask things that have already been covered. Some students drop what they really want to find out because they can't find it quickly. Other students are busily copying word for word out of sources that may or may not be appropriate.

Is this situation unique? Hardly. As a fifth-grade teacher we know said recently, "We have to teach it over and over and over." Despite exposure to instruction that should have helped them with research, many students have great difficulty with the research tasks schools expect them to perform. It is all too common, for example, to find students who can answer a direct question about some information-access feature, such as a table of contents, but who do not think to use such knowledge when they are actually trying to find information on their own. The knowledge just isn't available to them spontaneously.

> 66 *A*ny teacher who has observed a youngster demonstrate competence in a specific skill via a worksheet only to find the skill inaccessible during actual reading or writing knows the difference between learning a skill and being skillful. 99
>
> —STRICKLAND, 1994/1995, P. 297

Worse yet, some students simply get someone else to do the task for them. One of us, for example, recalls moving to a new school where she was impressed by the outstanding reports displayed on hallway bulletin boards. But when the children whose names were on those reports entered her classroom the next school year, it became clear that their parents had been largely responsible for the work.

We also noticed another big problem. In many elementary classrooms, students primarily read narrative texts. They are rarely exposed to nonfiction, including informational books. No wonder many students have trouble with reports and expository reading as they move into the upper grades!

> 66 *T*he narrative is especially pervasive in the elementary school curriculum. It has been estimated, in fact, that as much as 90% of what is read by elementary school children is narrative in form. 99
>
> —TRABASSO, 1994, P. 87

Some students rely on others to do their research reports.

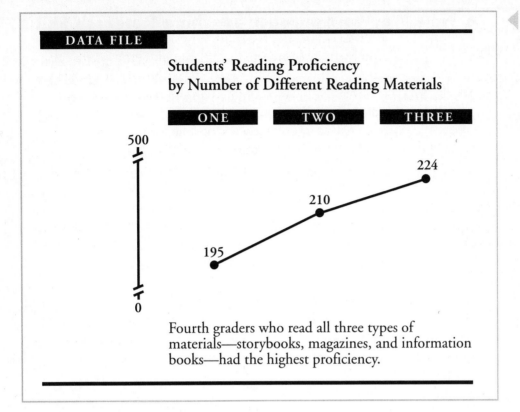

DATA FILE

Students' Reading Proficiency by Number of Different Reading Materials

| ONE | TWO | THREE |

195 210 224

Fourth graders who read all three types of materials—storybooks, magazines, and information books—had the highest proficiency.

The National Assessment of Educational Progress (NAEP) indicates that fourth graders' reading achievement increases as the diversity of their reported reading experience increases. In other words fourth graders who reported reading not only stories but also magazines and information books had the highest achievement. These NAEP findings also showed that students in the top third achieving schools nationwide reported reading more information books at school than students in the bottom third schools (Campbell, Kapinus, & Beatty, 1995).

This lack of exposure to information texts causes difficulty even for good readers, but the problem is particularly serious for less proficient readers, who have fewer opportunities to read nonfiction and perform research than do better readers. Without diverse reading experiences that include expository texts, students' ability to read and write effectively lags behind that of their better-read peers. We know, for example, that wide reading correlates with vocabulary development and general knowledge. And national data indicate that children who report diverse reading—including informational books—have higher reading achievement.

Research has established that wide reading correlates with vocabulary development and general knowledge in fourth to sixth graders, even when differences in general ability and phonological coding ability are controlled.

—CUNNINGHAM & STANOVICH, 1991

▲▲▲▲▲▲▲▲▲▲▲▲▲▲▲▲

Research Articles on Teaching Nonfiction

Looking for ways to increase the amount of nonfiction your students read? These short, easy-to-read resources will get you started.

◉ Doiron, R. (1994). **Using nonfiction in a read-aloud program: Letting the facts speak for themselves.** *The Reading Teacher, 47 (pp. 616–624).*

This article presents an annotated list of nonfiction books good for reading aloud to students. It also provides a list of eight points to remember in reading aloud.

◉ Dreher, M.J. (1998). **Motivating children to read more nonfiction.** *The Reading Teacher, 52 (pp. 414–417).*

This article shows how you can use simple reading logs to encourage more diverse reading during independent reading time.

◉ Sudol, P., and King, C. M. (1996). **A checklist for choosing nonfiction trade books.** *The Reading Teacher, 49 (pp. 422–424).*

This article offers specific criteria for selecting good information books to use in your classroom.

A New Way to Approach Teaching Research Skills

After considering many experiences like these, we wanted to change the way we taught students to research. We were concerned about students not really knowing how to approach a research task, not being able to apply what they had been "taught," and not having enough experience with nonfiction. We were concerned about less proficient readers having few research opportunities, and about students depending on teachers or parents, or feeling they could only succeed if they copied. So, a few years ago, we decided to concentrate our efforts on improving the situation.

We thought about the difficulties we had seen and what we might do to help students be more successful. We then worked collaboratively to identify instructional strategies to help our students improve their research skills; we implemented these strategies in elementary classrooms, refining what we did as we observed our students. We have experimented in classrooms for several years now, and have discovered that we have greatly improved our students' independence and motivation for research. Our ideas continue to evolve, and we hope yours will, too, as you think about and test the ideas we present here.

In the remaining part of this chapter, we will present an overview of our approach. The chapters that follow provide specific details and examples that will help you implement our techniques and strategies.

The Principles That Inform Our Model

In order to help students internalize the research process, we believe several important principles must be woven through all research activities. First, *students need direct instruction in reading and writing for research.* We recognize that being a good reader doesn't mean you are automatically a good researcher. Just because a student can read stories and textbooks well does not mean he or she will automatically be successful making decisions about resources, searching for information, and deciding what to include in notes. Reading to locate information, for example, involves different skills than reading stories and textbooks. Similarly all writing is not alike. Students who can write good stories cannot necessarily produce reports or posters or videos that integrate and summarize information from multiple sources. The differing demands require instructional attention. But even less proficient readers can be successful with research if provided with appropriate instruction and support.

Second, *students need research skills instruction that is meaningful.* This means that research skills need to be taught in the context of ongoing projects if the instruction is to be effective. We teach the skills as they are needed so that students make the link between the lessons and how they can

> **66** e award the highest academic accolade to a student who can see a question, focus it into an enquiry, trace sources, find relevant information in those sources, collate the information, reorganise that information in a way that meets the question posed, and write up the reorganised material as a report. To those who achieve that pinnacle of scholarship we award a Ph.D. This same process is the one we have adopted as the main teaching method for the less academic and less well-motivated school pupil...Yet we often give no specific help. **99**

—MARLAND, 1977, P. 208

Research Instruction Must Be Meaningful, or Else...

Dreher and Sammons (1994) asked fifth graders (all considered at least grade-level readers) to use a familiar-topic textbook to locate the answers to questions, all of which contained terms that could be looked up in the index. They found that the success rate was just more than 30%, most often because students did not think to use the index. Even those who did often looked up inappropriate terms or had trouble with alphabetical order. Unsuccessful researchers typically tried to locate the answers to the very specific questions by using the table of contents or paging through the text. Yet these students had been taught about indexes and other information-access features, and they could find the index and other features and explain their use when asked to do so.

Source: Dreher, M. J., and Sammons, R. B. (1994). Fifth graders' search for information in a textbook. *Journal of Reading Behavior, 26* (pp. 301–314).

actually be used in research. We identify the needed skills by noting the difficulties students encounter as they work. But even more important, we have students identify their own needs by reflecting on what they are doing. We say more about reflection later, and weave examples of contextualized instruction throughout the subsequent chapters.

Third, *students need many opportunities to engage in research.* Students won't become independent researchers unless they have lots of chances to apply what they have learned. Thus, during a school year, research activities should be ongoing—some activities short, some long, with varied approaches and products. As will be evident in the remaining chapters, reading, writing, and researching need to be an integral part of classroom activities. Further, we believe that many, varied research activities are important for all students, including less proficient readers. We give concrete examples of how to support mixed-ability groups of readers throughout the book.

Fourth, *students need differentiated instruction.* For some students delving into research questions, locating resources, note-taking, and developing other research skills is easy. But others require greater teacher support, and we have found that our approach makes it easy to differentiate instruction.

Fifth, *students need to be encouraged to reflect on the research process.* As an essential part of our effort to make instruction meaningful, we have students engage in daily reflection about their research activities. Both oral and written reflections are important because they encourage students' self-evaluation and ownership of their actions and build metacognition. We always ask students to share their successes and difficulties. We follow these collective shares with written "Reflections," as we show in Chapter 2. Students' comments during these reflection activities directly affect the instruction we provide.

Pulling It All Together

To make sure that research projects don't become mere assignments, we recommend a format we call "work sessions"; these sessions allow us to put our instructional principles into practice in the real world of the classroom. The chart below outlines a typical work session during a research project. Each work session involves instruction that is relevant to the unique demands of reading and writing for research. In addition this instruction is meaningful because it is rooted in the needs students have identified as they reflect on what they are doing.

Research Project
Daily Lesson Format for Work Sessions

ESTIMATED TIME	LESSON SECTION
5–10 min.	**MINI-LESSON** Each work period begins with a lesson focusing on a research process problem identified during a previous work session.
2 min.	**REVIEW RESEARCH MODEL** Each work period includes a review of the research process strategy model.
30–45 min.	**WORK PERIOD; NOTE PROBLEMS** Teacher notes students' problems as they work in order to identify mini-lesson topics. In selecting mini-lesson topics from these trouble spots, the teacher thinks in terms of the research objectives that have been identified for the grade level.
5–10 min.	**COLLECTIVE SHARE** Each work period ends with a collective share session in which students report what they tried, what worked, and what difficulties they had. The emphasis is on the research process. This share session provides another opportunity for the teacher to identify topics for future mini-lessons.
5–10 min.	**REFLECTION** Students write in "Reflections Books." Initially the teacher models writing reflections with group. The teacher monitors these Reflections Books to give students feedback as they develop their research skills; she also uses them to identify topics of future mini-lessons.

During a research project, a typical weekly pattern might be: (a) two periods of instruction during which the teacher guides students in learning social studies or science content via activities such as books, videos, discussion; and (b) three days of project work sessions in which students continue their conceptual development during research tasks. This pattern is shown in the next chart.

Typical Weekly Pattern

MONDAY	TUESDAY	WEDNESDAY	THURSDAY	FRIDAY
Mini-Lesson	Teacher-guided Social Studies or Science Instruction	Mini-Lesson	Teacher-guided Social Studies or Science Instruction	Mini-Lesson
Research Model Review		Research Model Review		Research Model Review
Project Work Period		Project Work Period		Project Work Period
Collective Share		Collective Share		Collective Share
Reflection		Reflection		Reflection

AGOP: A Research Model

What follows is a brief description of our model, which we explain fully in subsequent chapters. Using a research model guides instruction and helps students internalize the research process. It also helps students see the entire research process as a whole comprising many smaller parts. Students typically think of research as a product—usually a report—instead of a process. Indeed, when students are assigned a report, many are overwhelmed. They see only a large finished product looming; they often fail to see how lots of individual pieces contribute to the whole. So, we lead students to think about all the steps involved in a research project, which helps them envision the whole process.

You can invent an acronym for your own model. We call ours AGOP* for:

- Ask questions
- Gather information
- Organize and write
- Present

We use this research model as a guide that is posted in the classroom and referred to often. Here's how it works in practice:

1 Ask questions. To begin the research process, students choose a topic or develop the one their teacher gives them. Then they devise appropriate research questions to guide their quest. Although this step sounds straightforward, forming questions that are not too narrow and not too broad is a challenge for many students.

2 Gather information. As researchers seek answers to their questions, they gather information, which involves many complex operations. First, researchers must decide on what resources might contain the information they need. This process is often difficult for experienced researchers; it is particularly problematic for students who are not only unaware of many helpful resources but who also haven't developed a sense of what is in familiar resources. Once resources are selected, students must locate information in the source. They must remember about indexes and alphabetical order, tables of contents, skimming and scanning, headings, and about how different resources vary in their access features. Then, when students have located relevant information, they must apply their comprehension skills to understand that information. Then they must decide how to record the information.

3 Organize and write. After students locate information pertaining to their questions, they must figure out how to select and combine information from their notes and how to draft, revise, and edit their thoughts. These processes are difficult enough for students who are working with only one source, but the complexity skyrockets as older students are expected to locate and use multiple sources.

* The AGOP acronym has been in use by some teachers in Montgomery County Maryland Public Schools for many years to assist novice researchers, although our particular adaptation is unique.

We have not been able to determine who originated this acronym.

4   **Present.** At this point students present their findings. In our view research projects should always involve some form of presentation. A presentation helps ensure that the research project involves all aspects of the communicative arts (reading, writing, speaking, listening). To make an effective presentation, students select an appropriate type of presentation and prepare a visual aid to support it.

Students go through the AGOP steps in a somewhat sequential order. But the nature of research means that students may cycle through these steps more than once as they encounter problems. As students begin to gather information, for example, they may need to back up and adjust their questions. Similarly, as they try to organize their notes, they may find that they need to go back and gather more information.

Research supports the effectiveness of the systematic instruction discussed in this book. In a yearlong study at two very different schools (one with a predominantly white, middle-income population and the other with a predominantly minority population and substantial Title I funding), Dreher et al. used the AGOP model and Reflections Logs (see Chapter 2) to provide instruction in meaningful context. These researchers found that at both schools students improved at a statistically significant level in searching for information, writing answers to research questions, and applying what they had learned to a new situation.

—DREHER ET AL., 1998

Looking Ahead

In the rest of this book, we give you the details and many examples of how to use our AGOP model, in conjunction with our instructional principles, to scaffold your students toward becoming independent researchers. In Chapter 2 we begin by explaining a very important part of making instruction meaningful—having your students reflect on their research. We show you how to encourage reflection and what kind of information you get when you do so. Then, in the remaining chapters, we show you how to use your students' reflections to take them through the four steps of the model: Asking questions, Gathering information, Organizing and writing, and Presenting.

2

Making Instruction Meaningful

Most of this book is devoted to showing you how to help your students *ask questions, gather information, organize and write,* and *present.* But simply teaching them these four steps won't result in students automatically knowing how to research. If your students are to become independent researchers, they need instruction that helps them internalize research skills. A critical part of providing your students with such instruction is to make it meaningful. We have found that we can make research meaningful by encouraging self-evaluation and ownership. We do this by having students reflect on what they are doing at each stage of the research process. Then we use students' reflections to design our instruction. In this chapter we show you how to have your students reflect on their work, and we explain why this is so important. In the following chapters, we will show you how students' reflections lead directly to instruction at each stage of the research process.

Using Reflections Logs

As we indicated in Chapter 1, at the close of each work session we have students briefly share their successes and difficulties. As the teacher you will actively participate in this discussion. You might share what you noticed as your students worked. Perhaps you noticed a student encountering a common problem or figuring out how to solve a difficulty. You might draw out insights from students that will be meaningful to others in your classroom.

After sharing their experiences, students then engage in written reflections, using "Reflections Logs" like the one shown on the following page. Our Reflections Log helps students revisit their research experiences during a work session. This Reflections Log has four sections, and each section serves an important purpose.

Getting the Most Out of Reflection Logs

The *first section* asks students to think about what parts of the research process they engaged in that day. During a given session, students may work on multiple parts of the research process, so in this section they may often check more than one category. By thinking about the many parts that contribute to the whole as they conduct research, students begin to see research as a process, not as a product.

The *second section* asks students to recall what activities they actually engaged in that day. Students can write a brief description or draw and label their activities, and they can continue on the back of the page if they need more space. (The drawing option will be helpful to your struggling readers and writers, but some of your most capable students will also find this option appealing.) Reflecting on what they did is the first step in evaluating the effectiveness of their actions in the remaining portion of the Reflections Log.

In the *third and fourth sections* of the log, students evaluate their successes and difficulties. These sections encourage students to engage in metacognitive thinking about their strengths and needs. Such thinking is important in helping students become independent learners.

Some students find it hard to admit they are having any problems with their research. This is especially true for older children and for those who have a history of difficulty in reading. Keeping this in mind, we worded the third and fourth sections of the Reflections Log in a nonthreatening way. For

Name _____ Date _____

Reflections

1 What part(s) of the research process were you working on today?

___ forming research questions

___ searching for resources

___ locating information in a resource

___ taking notes

___ organizing information

___ drafting

___ revising

___ publishing

___ polishing (graphics, visuals, plays, etc.)

___ presenting

___ evaluating

___ other (tell what _____)

2 How did you do that part of the research process today? Write or draw what you did.

3 What was hard about that part of the research process today?

What was easy about that part of the research process today?

4 I think a good topic for the next lesson would be _____

_____

because _____ .

Easy Steps to Writing Fantastic Research Reports · Scholastic Professional Books

example, section 3 asks students to report both "hard" parts and "easy" parts, and they can leave the "hard" part blank. Similarly the wording in section 4 allows a student to suggest a topic for the next lesson because he or she is having trouble with it; but the student can also suggest lessons for other reasons, such as seeing others experience some sort of problem.

You can see that the Reflections Log asks students to think about some very important processes, yet it is short and carefully focused so filling it out doesn't become a chore. There is just enough writing on our Reflections Log to accomplish our purpose of getting students to think about what they are doing, how it all fits together, and what they still need to know.

Pinpointing Students' Needs

We think the best way to document the value of Reflections Logs is to show you examples of the kind of information you can get from your students' logs.

Asking the Right Questions

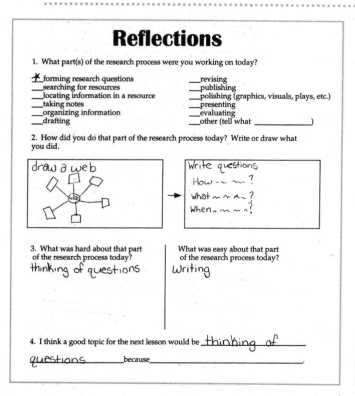

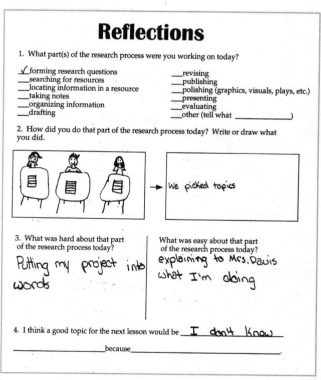

In these Reflections Logs, you can see students' comments about the difficulty of forming research questions. (The figure in the top left box of the log on the left is a drawing of a graphic organizer we use to help support students as they form research questions. You will find similar organizers in Chapter 3.) These logs, from one of the first research projects in the school year, accurately capture how difficult it is for students to pose questions at the right level. Indeed, we have found that many students ask questions that are too narrow. Although we can have general discussions about how to pose appropriate questions, activities aimed at this problem are more meaningful when students themselves experience this problem firsthand. In Chapter 3 we detail an example lesson to help students handle this challenge.

Reflections

1. What part(s) of the research process were you working on today?

___ forming research questions
___ searching for resources
✓ locating information in a resource
✓ taking notes
___ organizing information
___ drafting

___ revising
___ publishing
___ polishing (graphics, visuals, plays, etc.)
___ presenting
___ evaluating
___ other (tell what _____)

2. How did you do that part of the research process today? Write or draw what you did.

| I looked in the table of contents of the Tidewater Indians. | → | I found lots of things in lots of diffient catagories |

3. What was hard about that part of the research process today?

Finding the resource that was best for the information I needed

What was easy about that part of the research process today?

Looking in the table of contents

4. I think a good topic for the next lesson would be __what books are the best for__ because __I couldn't find one__ the infomation I need

Reflections

1. What part(s) of the research process were you working on today?

___ forming research questions
___ searching for resources
✓ locating information in a resource
✓ taking notes
___ organizing information
___ drafting

___ revising
___ publishing
___ polishing (graphics, visuals, plays, etc.)
___ presenting
___ evaluating
___ other (tell what _____)

2. How did you do that part of the research process today? Write or draw what you did.

| First we went on the computer and we got nothing. | → | Then we looked in the book called Tidewater Indians and we got a lot OF information. |

3. What was hard about that part of the research process today?

locating a resource

What was easy about that part of the research process today?

finding information in the resource

4. I think a good topic for the next lesson would be __Knowing what is a resource__ because __so you don't have to waste your time by looking everywhere.__ good

Reflections

1. What part(s) of the research process were you working on today?

___ forming research questions
___ searching for resources
✓ locating information in a resource
✓ taking notes
___ organizing information
___ drafting

___ revising
___ publishing
___ polishing (graphics, visuals, plays, etc.)
___ presenting
___ evaluating
___ other (tell what _____)

2. How did you do that part of the research process today? Write or draw what you did.

| I use the book the Indians of the Northeast. | → | It helped a lot it was a great book to help find the answers |

3. What was hard about that part of the research process today?

Trying to find the book that I needed

What was easy about that part of the research process today?

looking in the index and reading the part that I needed.

4. I think a good topic for the next lesson would be __telling me where they are located__ because __so I won't look in the wrong book.__

In these three Reflections, students note that it was hard to find the right resource for the kind of information they needed. These students want to know the types of information that can be found in different kinds of resources and where those resources can be found in the media center and the classroom. In Chapter 4 we show an example lesson to help students handle this type of problem.

Using an Index

Here a student expresses her frustration with index conventions. She was using a trade book to find information on a certain type of whale. She complained to her teacher about the index because, after consulting it, she had looked on every page from 19 to 54 and had only found two pieces of information. When her teacher asked the girl to show her the index, the teacher realized the problem: The index entry read "19, 54" rather than "19–54." If the student had understood index conventions, she would have looked only on pages 19 and 54. Even though this student had completed worksheets on index conventions in previous classes, she did not internalize the information because it was meaningless to her. Now that she needs the information, she is ready to learn it. We show you how you can help with index problems in Chapter 4.

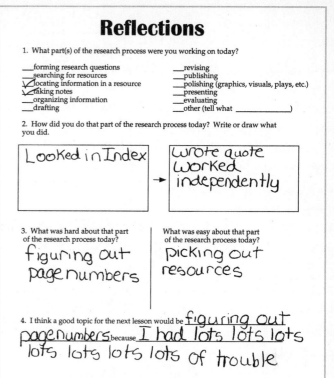

Taking Notes

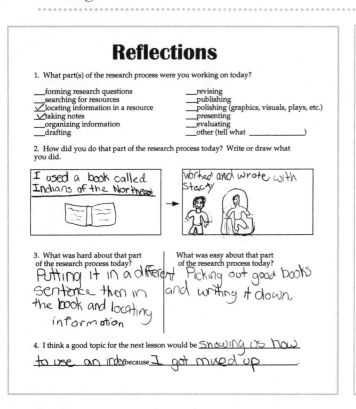

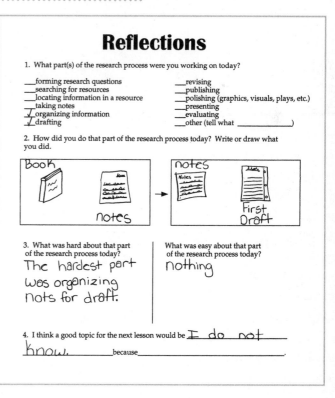

The example on the left shows how you can get instructional feedback from sections 3 and 4 of the Reflections Log. This student continues to seek additional help with indexes (section 4), but she also notes in section 3 how hard it was for her to put the information she found into her own words. "Using your own words" when note-taking is a common problem. In addition, as the example on the right indicates, students find it difficult to organize their notes to write a first draft. We talk about helping students use their own words and organize their drafts in Chapter 5.

You can see from these examples what a wealth of information your students' Reflections will give you about the difficulties they are having. You will find that many of the lessons your students have been exposed to simply haven't "stuck." However, if you provide mini-lessons on problems that students themselves have identified, you will see that the lessons do stick with them. Indeed, we have found students pay close attention to a lesson "Brought to you by Diana!" or "By special request from Mark!" In the following chapters, we show how you to create mini-lessons.

▲ Kate's students write entries in their Reflections Books.

Making "Reflections Books"

Although you can use individual Reflections Logs with your students, we believe these logs are most powerful if each student has a book compiling his or her logs. We bind Reflections Logs into a spiral book of about 50 pages, with a cover and a table of contents. The example at the top of page 21 shows a cover page we have used for our Reflections Book in the fourth grade. This cover page shows a crab, which we have named AGOP; the crab sees the research model components reflected in the water. (You are not obligated to use our crab mascot unless you happen to be studying Maryland's fourth-grade curriculum, too!) In addition, we include a table of contents, also shown on page 21. We have students add a new entry to their table of contents as they start each new research project.

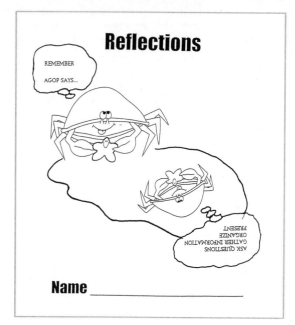

Reflections

REMEMBER

AGOP SAYS...

ASK QUESTIONS
GATHER INFORMATION
ORGANIZE
PRESENT

Name _____

Table of Contents

Having the Reflections Logs bound together allows students to review and reflect later in the term on their earlier concerns. Doing so is another aspect of self-evaluation. For example, at right is a student's response midway through the semester, when she was asked to look back over her entries and think about what she had learned about finding information.

You can ask your students to reread their Reflections entries periodically and set goals for themselves. For example, at the end of a project, you might distribute a form like the one at right.

To encourage students to look back over their progress, you can insert a sheet at regular intervals in each student's Reflections Book. The example on page 22 should be inserted after every tenth Reflections Log.

> You should look in the index of your book first so you don't waste time looking at every page in the book when the index will tell you what page the subject is on.

You have just completed your research project on Ancient Rome. Now look back over the Reflections Logs you wrote during your project. What did you learn about doing research during this project? What do you want to know more about to improve your research skills?

_____
_____
_____
_____
_____
_____
_____
_____
_____
_____
_____

Name _____ Date _____

You Have Just Completed
10 Reflections!

Now look back over those 10 entries and answer the following questions.

1 What were two problems that you encountered?

_____

_____

_____

_____

2 What did you learn about how to solve those problems?

_____

_____

_____

_____

3 What research skills do you want to improve in the next few projects?

_____

_____

_____

_____

Easy Steps to Writing Fantastic Research Reports   Scholastic Professional Books

Making Reflections Logs Work

Modeling How to Use the Logs

To help students learn how to fill out their Reflections Logs, we model the process. We use an overhead projector to display a blank Reflections Log so that all students can see it. One technique we use is *shared writing*—we ask students to describe their activities during a research session, and then have them assist us as we record what they experienced. Another technique we use is to think aloud about our own experiences during a research task; we then ask our students to help us complete the log based on what we reported. We find that most students quickly understand the task after two or three modeling sessions.

MINI-LESSON

Introducing the Reflections Book and Modeling the Use of a Reflections Log

PURPOSE

To model for students how to think about their research and record their thoughts.

In this lesson Kate introduces Reflections Books. She then shows her students how to complete Reflections Logs based on their analysis of the work they have just completed. They have just begun a research project on Tidewater Indians. Today they are looking at potential books for their topic. Kate has just had her students share what they tried, what worked, and what difficulties they experienced. Now Kate introduces the Reflections Books and Logs.

MATERIALS

- overhead projector
- marker
- transparencies of a Reflections Book cover and a Reflections Log
  (or chart paper with Reflections Log written on it)

PRESENTING THE LESSON

Kate: Well, it is obvious that you've all worked very hard this period. Your comments were very good. I like the way you thought back over what you did today. When you think back over what you've done and evaluate how it went, we call that *reflecting on your work.* Your reflections about your work can be very valuable because they can help you identify good ways to do things, things that didn't work too well, and important skills you need to learn more about.

In a minute I'm going to show you a form we will be using this year to help you reflect on your research work. But first I'm going to introduce you to a friend of mine named AGOP. [Kate puts a transparency of the cover of the Reflections Book on the overhead.] What's AGOP doing?

Jackie: Looking in the water at himself.

Kate: Yes, he is looking at his reflection. What is he thinking about?

Luis: He's thinking, Ask questions, gather, organize, and present.

Kate: That's right. Those are all the steps in the research process.

Kate explains that AGOP decorates the cover of a book in which they will record their reflections about research. She then shows the class a transparency of a REFLECTIONS LOG.

Kate: I'll bet you aren't surprised to see that the title of the form is "Reflections." Today we'll fill out this form together. Later this week you will start doing your own Reflections Logs! You can see that this Reflections Log has four sections. Let's look at the first section. Sarah, would you read the first question for us?

Sarah: "What part of the research process were you working on today?"

Bryan: Oh, we were finding good books for our research.

Kate: Great. So I'll put a check by that on our Reflections. Paul, would you read the next question?

Paul: "How did you do that part of the research process today? Write or draw what you did."

Kate: Okay. This part lets us write or draw about what we did. Sometimes students write and draw, even making up a cartoon with writing in it. What do you think we should put in the box for today?

Jess: You could draw pictures of some books.

Paul: You could write, "We looked for good books."

Sarah: "We found lots of books."

Kate: All good ideas. I think I'll draw a picture of some books in the first box and write "We tried to find good books" in the second box. We only needed two boxes today. But if you need to, you can continue on the back. Now let's move on to the third section. Reiko, will you read the questions for us?

Reiko: "What was hard about that part of the research process today? What was easy about that part of the research process today?"

Kate: Thank you. Now let's think back to our discussion. What were some of the things you thought were hard to do today?

Mike: Looking at indexes.

Jane: Finding books on our topic.

Kate: Good. I'll record those points here on the left side. Now were there things you felt were pretty easy?

Lisa: Reading titles.

Paul: Looking at pictures.

Kate: Okay. I'll record those points here on the right side. Jason, would you read the last section for us?

Jason: "I think a good topic for tomorrow's mini-lesson would be..."

Kate: Now we need to think back over our answers and decide what might be a good lesson for next time. We have a list of what we did, what we thought was easy, and what we thought was hard. We can use that information to help us decide on a lesson that might be helpful. What do you think?

The students decide they need to know how to select the right materials. They want to know how they can tell if a book will really help them find the information they want.

Kate: That's a really good idea. Before our next research session, why don't I teach you a strategy that helps you find the right book?

Kate does another group lesson at the end of the next work session modeling the use of the Reflections Log. Most students can then proceed independently. Kate provides individual help if certain students need it.

Encouraging Students to Ask Questions

In addition to modeling how to use these Reflections Logs, we make sure that during research work sessions we convey to our students the importance of asking questions. When students encounter problems and ask for help, we routinely provide suggestions and assistance. But we also emphasize the value of their questions. For example you will often hear us make remarks such as, "Sabrina, that's an excellent topic for the next mini-lesson. I'm sure a lot of other kids are wondering about that, too. Why not include it on your Reflections page?" Why do we do this? If we do not help our students take note of their questions and discoveries, they tend not to remember them. Consequently, they are not likely to seek out answers to their questions or share their triumphs. By giving them such feedback, we help students become more reflective on their strengths and weaknesses in the search processes and encourage them to become active, inquisitive, independent learners.

Also, our feedback highlights the importance of asking questions—a critical concept because many students assume that if they ask a question, it means they are not capable. Recently, for example, one of us was working with sixth graders at a school whose students were not involved in our program; the task was to gather data on what these students did on their own during a short research assignment. As part of the project, students had a log sheet to track any questions they asked. But many students simply did not want to acknowledge that they asked anybody anything. They did not want anyone to jot down the questions they asked, as though it were wrong to ask questions! In contrast, our emphasis on reflection helps illustrate to students that their questions are not something to hide but instead are important feedback for themselves and their teachers.

Looking Ahead

The examples in this chapter show how you can use Reflections Logs to identify students' difficulties. In the next chapters, we will show you how to move your students through the four steps of the research process. As we do so, you will find examples of how to use the information from Reflections Logs to create meaningful instruction at each step.

Asking Questions

In this chapter we focus on the *A* in AGOP—*asking questions.* If you want your students to be motivated and successful, it is very important that the questions they investigate are meaningful to them, and that they learn to ask "good" questions—questions that are not too narrow and not too broad. In this chapter we discuss how you can involve your students so that they are interested in their research topics, and we show you how you can help them formulate good research questions. We also provide examples of how to use your students' Reflections Logs to plan your mini-lessons.

To make the questions your students investigate compelling to them, forge a strong connection between the research/writing task and high-interest curriculum areas, such as science and social studies. By doing so you provide your students with an authentic situation within which to practice and refine their research skills. This isn't a research skill being taught in isolation. This isn't a ditto from an English book. This isn't a scavenger hunt in the media center. Rather, it is instruction linked to a real task.

To get the research process going, you will help your students learn to ask questions. How can they access information if they can't figure out exactly what they would like to know? Your job will be to help them focus their inquiries. You will help them formulate questions that are meaty enough for research.

Selecting a Topic for Research

The questioning process really begins with the selection of the topic. Involve your students as much as possible. Give them choices. How you handle this phase of the process can make or break a project before it even begins. Strike a balance between what you want them to gain from their research and their own personal interests. By giving them a say, you stimulate interest and give your students a sense of ownership of the project.

Integrating Research Into Your Curriculum

In order to clarify our ideas, we will use specific examples from Kate's classroom. In her classroom research topics are always linked to social studies and science. In science her fourth-grade students study ecosystems, rocks and minerals, and electricity. Her social studies curriculum focuses on the study of the state of Maryland. Units cover the geography, history, government, and economy of the state.

When Kate began teaching this grade level, she too was learning the curriculum, so she decided it was best to start small. Because her class was studying oceans as part of a unit on ecosystems, and because whales live in the ocean and are of great interest to intermediate students, she chose whales as the first research project. Kate showed *The Voyage of the MiMi* (Sunburst Corporation), a content-rich video program that talks about the migratory habits of humpback whales, to provide some background knowledge on whales and build students' motivation for learning more about them. The video came with a large poster depicting the various whale species; Kate hung the poster on the wall and asked students to select a whale they'd like to learn more about. Students then were invited to research the whale they had chosen.

Kate kept the main topic of the project small by having all her students work on whales. There were enough different species of whales, however, to give her students many options. The project was a success and it was manageable. It was easy for her to check the accuracy of the information contained in the students' work because they were basically writing about one subject.

As time passed and Kate's knowledge of the curriculum content grew, so did the scope of the projects she assigned her students. The following chart illustrates how topics have flowed from the curriculum and been expanded upon. The chart contains examples of projects she has assigned over the years. *On average each project takes from two to five weeks to complete.*

Examples of Research Project Topics

SCIENCE

Ecosystems

- Whales
- Marine Mammals
- Chesapeake Bay
- Wetlands
- Salt Marsh Communities

Rocks & Minerals

- Gems
- Volcanoes
- Plate Tectonics
- Designing a Display for the Museum of Natural History in Washington, D.C.

Electricity

- Inventors/Inventions
- Biography
- Science Applications
- Lightning
- Safety Considerations
- Power Sources
- Local Power Companies

Continued on next page

Continued from page 29

SOCIAL STUDIES

Geography

- Land Formations
- Erosion
- Chesapeake Drainage Basin
- Continental Divide
- Regions
- Washington, D.C.
- Baltimore, Maryland
- Maryland Counties

History

- First Marylanders (Native Americans)
- Early Settlement
- Colonial Settlement
- Slaves and Indentured Servants
- French and Indian War
- Revolutionary War
- War of 1812
- Civil War
- Women's History
- Immigration

Economy

- Plantations
- Colonial Craftsmen

Government

- Candidates Running for National Office
- Candidates Running for Local Office
- State Government
- Local Government
- County Seats

As you can see, Kate's list of possible research topics has grown substantially since that first whale report she assigned, and it is still growing! Kate varies the research topics from year to year. The following box contains a list of topics and the time frame for them in a typical school year.

Overview of One Year's Research Projects in Kate Davis's Classroom

Approximate Time Line	Selected Research Projects	Resources & Products
September (4 weeks)	**Geography of Maryland**	**Resources:** Textbooks and posters **Products:** Overlay map of Maryland
October–November (6-8 weeks)	**Maryland Indians** (First written report. Emphasis placed on research process.)	**Resources:** Textbooks, library books, posters, Native American travel trunk, speakers, CD-ROM **Products:** Written report consisting of at least six paragraphs and visual (art/crafts project)
December (4 weeks)	**Whales**	**Resources:** Textbooks, library books, videos, web sites, posters, CD-ROM **Products:** Written report and papier-mâché model
February (4 weeks)	**Black History** (Focus on Marylanders)	**Resources:** Textbooks, library books, biography, videos, maps **Product:** Written report
March (5 weeks)	**Women's "Herstory"**	**Resources:** Interview, review of oral histories **Product:** Video or audiotape of interview
April (4 weeks)	**County Reports**	**Resources:** Encyclopedia, travel brochures, library books, web sites **Products:** Travel brochure and TV commercials
May (5 weeks)	**Maryland Wax Museum**	**Resources:** Previous products, textbooks, encyclopedia, biographies **Product:** Wax museum with vignettes
June (2 weeks)	**State Symbols**	**Resources:** Library books, web sites **Products:** Poster and short report

The following mini-lesson demonstrates how students can take an active role in determining a research topic within the realm of the curriculum. Within the broad scope of *ecosystems,* Kate narrowed the topic to whales; her students further narrowed it to a particular species of whale.

MINI-LESSON

Narrowing the Topic

PURPOSE

To involve students in the selection of a research topic by having them brainstorm in groups and then collectively share ideas on narrowing broad topics.

MATERIALS

- large Marine Mammal Chart
- chart paper
- markers
- commercial charts containing facts about ecosystems

BEFORE THE MINI-LESSON

Prior to this lesson, students in Kate's class had studied ecosystems for several weeks and had become interested in the humpback whale.

PRESENTING THE LESSON

Kate begins by reviewing what comprises an ecosystem. She leads her students in a discussion of the ocean as an ecosystem. She explains to her class that over the next four weeks they will be researching whales as part of their study of ecosystems. She explains that the subject, *whales,* is far too large a topic to research.

She suggests that the class begin to focus their study by classifying whales into their two main scientific classifications, the suborders "toothed" and "baleen." To make the task even more manageable, students will need to narrow the subject further by selecting only one species of whale to research. Kate then proceeds as follows:

1. Kate explains that students may select any whale they want to study. She also tells them they may work together in groups to gather information about their whale.

2. She suggests they use the marine mammal chart (that came with *The Voyage of the MiMi* video program) to help them select the type of whale they wish to study. She asks, "Using the chart, what type of whale do you think it would be fun to research?"

3. After students have a chance to use the chart and talk over their ideas with their classmates, Kate makes a chart of all the whale types the class is interested in. She has students help her determine whether to list each whale on the chart under "toothed" or "baleen," so students can see which whales belong to the same suborder.

4. She concludes by discussing how students focused their research task by choosing a species. Rather than take on a broad topic, such as whales, students identified the main groups (baleen and toothed) into which whales are classified, and then chose a species from one group. She draws the following visual on the chalkboard:

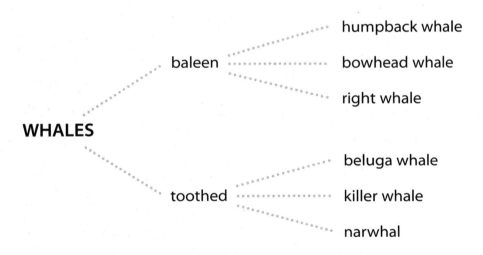

By allowing her students to select what they wished to research from broad areas, as illustrated in the preceding mini-lesson, Kate enabled her class to feel motivated by their interest and empowered by their choice. Within the broad parameters of your own school's curriculum, students will be able to select topics that are of high interest to them. This makes for the perfect blend of choice and manageability.

Sharpening the Research Focus

Once you have defined the broad research topic, your students need to choose their specific topic and generate research questions. You can help your novice researchers select good topics and generate good research questions by first assessing their prior knowledge of the subject and then stimulating their interest. What do they already know? What do they want to find out? A large-group activity in which all students are encouraged to share their background knowledge is an excellent way to begin. You can record this information on the chalkboard or on charts, and then compile it for your students on a handout for all to share. For example, at the beginning of a research project on whales, Kate's students listed what they knew (some of it incorrect) about whales.

> Whales are big fish.
> Whales live in the ocean.
> Whales are as big as a school bus.
> Whales weigh 5,000 pounds.
> Whales shoot water out of their heads.
> Whales kill sharks.
> Whales can attack boats.
> Whales have huge teeth.

Compiling what your students already know helps in two ways. First, it provides them with a knowledge base from which to proceed and to which they can refer if necessary during their research. Second, it serves as a diagnostic tool for you to assess your class's prior knowledge and, therefore, gives you some idea as to where to go next. It may even determine whether you have students investigate a particular subject. If students already know a lot about the subject, there may be no point in pursuing it further.

Sparking Student Interest

If the subject area is one for which the students have little or no background knowledge, you will need to add the extra step of introducing some information before you begin. You can do this through the use of films, videos, reading assignments, specially designed lessons, etc. Whatever activities you choose, they should be full to the brim with information in order to arouse students' curiosity and stimulate the questioning process.

Students need at least *some* background information to generate questions about a research topic. There are many different ways of stimulating interest and making sure your students have the background knowledge they need to pose research questions. Here are some approaches you can use.

Making Posters to Build Background Knowledge

When Kate wanted her students to research colonial craftsmen for a report on the economic factors that were an influence during the colonial period in Maryland, she ran into two problems with the research task. First, her students didn't have enough background information about occupations that provided products and services during this period. Second, they did not understand the principles that drive an economy.

Kate realized students needed more background information before they could pick their research topic (i.e., which craftsman they would like to study in depth). They also needed more information about economic influences at the time in order to determine where they wanted their research to lead them. Without this information, they simply could not be expected to develop good research questions.

Kate put students in groups to make posters showing the different colonial craftsmen in their workshops, from pictures she provided. They then presented their posters to the rest of the class, describing the people they had placed in their picture, the materials being used, the tools they saw the craftsmen using, and the products/services they saw being produced.

By making posters, copied from pictures in a colonial coloring book, students become aware of the equipment and materials necessary in each colonial workshop. What tools were needed? Who worked there? What did they make? How were products and services advertised?

This collaborative activity provided the students with the background knowledge they needed about colonial occupations and the four economic cornerstones Kate expected them to include in their reports: human resources, capital resources, natural resources, and products/services. Students had a great time making the posters and were loaded with the information they needed to choose a craftsman and formulate their research questions.

Exploring Textbooks to Motivate Students

Many knowledge-building activities serve to stimulate student interest by piquing curiosity. If students genuinely want to know more about a topic, they will approach the research process with energy and enthusiasm; they will be completing the task for themselves just as much as for you.

Encouraging students to look critically at their textbooks and question editorial decisions can be a big motivator. Before asking students to do a report on "Women's Herstory," in which students would consider the role of women in the state's history, Kate wanted to stimulate students' interest in the topic. She used the students' textbook, *Our Maryland* (3rd edition, by Jane Eagen and Jeanne McGinnis, Salt Lake City: Peregrine Smith Books, 1996) to generate interest in finding out about women in history. She asked students to examine the entries in the book's index and tabulate the entries for men and those for women.

Students examine the index of their social studies book, identifying entries for men and for women.

Students then use their math skills to tally and chart the entries for each sex. The paucity of entries for women motivated students to question how women and other groups are represented in textbooks.

When students compared the number of entries for men with the number for women, they discovered the lack of representation of women in their book. This activity sparked a good deal of discussion. Why were there so few entries in the book? Was it due to the lack of contributions made by women, or the lack of giving them proper credit for what they had done? This discussion led students to consider the underrepresentation of some groups in traditional history books. Kate introduced the concept of oral history as an important source of historical information.

Students, eager to fill in the gaps noted in their history book, then interviewed older, interesting women in their lives to compile an "oral herstory." These interviews helped address some of the questions raised about the underrepresentation of women in the textbook. It was great fun and many families extended the project by interviewing all their older family members.

**FAMOUS NAMES
IN MARYLAND HISTORY**

Name:_____

Date:_____

1. Use the dates given in the title of Chapter 3 and the copyright information in the front of the book to determine how many years of history are covered in your text. _____years.

2. Use the index in the back of your textbook to make a tally of all the names that are listed on the chart below.

Men	Women	Not Sure

3. Use your tally sheet to list the results of your findings.
    - Total names listed in the index:_____
    - Total of Men listed:_____
    - Total of Women Listed:_____
    - Total of names you were Not Sure of:_____

OUR MARYLAND   Jane Eagen and Jeanne McGinnis

4. Use the data you have tallied to construct the circle graph below.

Title:_____

Key:
Men ◯
Women ◯
Not Sure ◯

5. Explain what your graph show. What can you conclude from the data you have collected about the role of men and women in Maryland History?_____
_____
_____
_____
_____
_____
_____

More Activities That Motivate Students

There are many other ways to generate student interest in a topic and give them the background they need to formulate questions. The ideas listed below can easily make students want to find out more!

Field Trips

- Maryland Science Center
- Smithsonian Institute
- Baltimore Aquarium
- Historic St. Mary's City
- Williamsburg, Virginia

Guest Speakers

- Local Scientist (many parents are available to talk about what they do)
- Living History Performer (museum outreach programs)

Performance Tasks

- Colonial Crafts and Games
- Native American Crafts and Games
- Preparing Recipes
- Hands-on Science Experiments

Videos and Films

- Science
- Social Studies

One activity that worked well in Kate's class was having her students explore and complete activities from a Traveling Outreach Trunk she obtained from the Maryland Historical Society. Kits like this contain items usually found in a museum and are designed to provide students with a hands-on museum experience in the classroom.

Kate's class most recently used a Traveling Outreach Trunk titled *Many Homelands, One New Home: Immigration to Maryland.* This kit contained reproductions of historic artifacts, slides, photographs, documents, and oral history tapes depicting immigration to Maryland from the 1600s to the present day. The trunk inspired many questions about what might cause people to leave their homeland and move to a new country. The questions the students generated led to an exploration of their own families' histories and ethnic heritage.

Kate's students have also explored the contents of *Forgotten Folks: Maryland Indians*, a traveling trunk from the Maryland Historical Society. One group of students spontaneously generated questions on the topic of Tidewater Indians' clothing, including,

- How did the Indians get the hides so soft? (The skins feel like velvet.)
- How did you put the clothing on?
- How did the clothing fasten?
- How was the clothing the boys wore different from the girls?
- What was the "fringe" for?
- What did other decorations look like? For the boys? For the girls?

Hands-on activities, such as field trips or traveling trunks, capture students' attention and make them want to find out more about a topic.

Students' curiosity is aroused and many questions are generated by exploring the contents of a travelling trunk, *Forgotten Folks: Maryland Indians*, from the Maryland Historical Society.

Formulating Research Questions

O nce you have assessed your students' background knowledge or introduced the information they need to select specific research topics, you are ready to help them formulate research questions. Novice researchers tend to ask questions that are far too narrow and specific to make an interesting report. Often their questions can be answered in one word (e.g., "What color is a killer whale?" or "How many people worked in a colonial apothecary?" or "How many gods did the Romans worship?"). If you point out this problem, many students will understand what you mean, but they may still have difficulty fixing the problem on their own.

Turning "Little Questions" Into "Big Questions"

To help children formulate appropriate research questions, we model how to organize their "little questions" into groups of related questions. Once little questions are grouped together, broader categories that are very researchable begin to emerge. We call these categories the "big questions." Little questions—such as *What color is a whale?* or *How much does it weigh?* or *What does the pattern on its flukes look like?*—translate into the big question, *What are the physical characteristics of a humpback whale?* That big question will be answered when your students have located the answers to all the little questions. Big questions lend themselves very well to writing an interesting report. They are big or broad enough to be studied and written about. It's the big questions we want our students to be good at formulating.

M I N I - L E S S O N

Identifying Good Questions

PURPOSE

The following mini-lesson is designed to help students formulate big questions to use during their research. Specifically you have students brainstorm questions and then show them how little questions can be categorized into big questions.

MATERIALS

- highlighters
- black fine-tip markers
- colored sentence strips
- chart paper
- masking tape

Kate asked students to brainstorm questions about colonial craftsmen and complete the web shown at right.

Kate collected the completed webs and looked them over. She then highlighted at least one question on each web for students to share during the mini-lesson. She used markers in four different colors so that all the questions she highlighted in the same color pertained to the same category (Products and Services, Natural Resources, Capital Resources, Human Resources). For example, Kate used blue to highlight "What products do they make?" on the web below.

Kate was able to categorize all the students' questions into the four main topics for the research project. Everyone wrote at least one good question they were invited to share. Everyone contributed to the process.

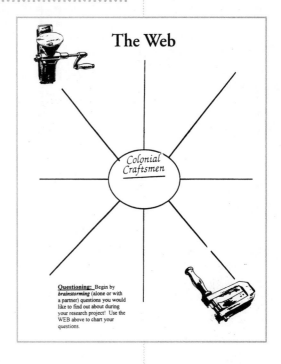

The Web

Colonial Craftsmen

Questioning: Begin by *brainstorming* (alone or with a partner) questions you would like to find out about during your research project! Use the WEB above to chart your questions.

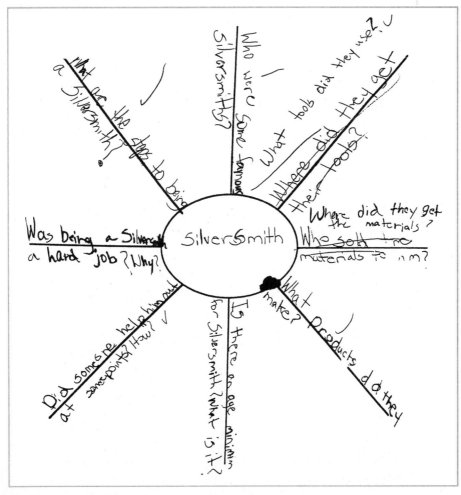

The Web

Write your research topic in the circle. Then brainstorm questions you would like to find out about during your research. Write your questions on the lines coming out of the circle.

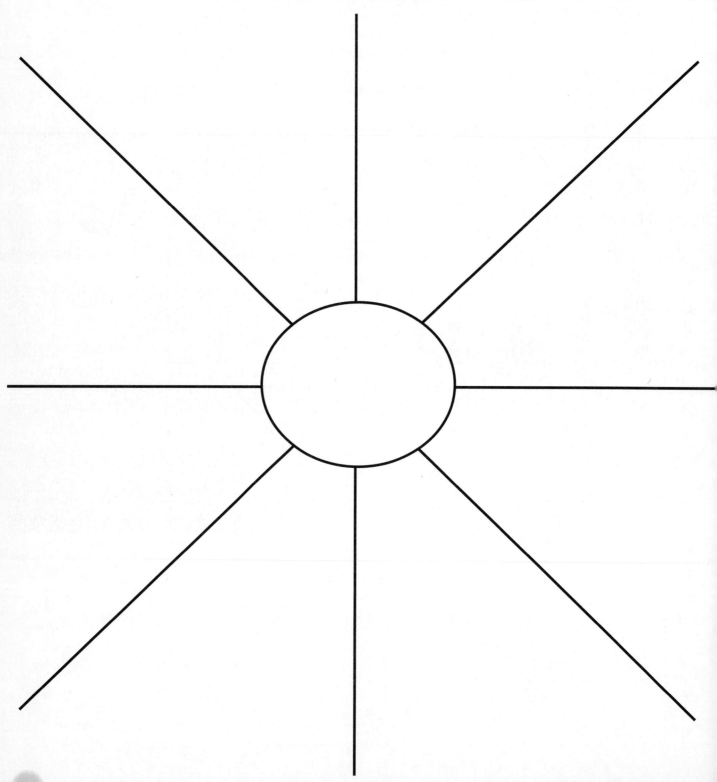

Easy Steps to Writing Fantastic Research Reports   Scholastic Professional Book

1. Kate compliments students on their excellent questions and invites them to share their questions with the rest of the class.

2. She hands back their webs and asks students to copy the question she has highlighted on a color-coded sentence strip with fine-tip markers. The color of the sentence strip matches the color Kate used to highlight the question on the student's web.

3. While her students copy their questions onto the sentence strips, Kate divides the chalkboard into sections using masking tape.

Students organize their questions into categories. They soon discover that categories become "big questions." Finding the answer to the "little questions" will provide them with details they need to write about their big questions.

Once students identify the "big questions," Kate posts them on a chart for students to consult.

4. Kate asks students to read their questions aloud and then place them on the board. The graphic organizers on page 44 illustrate how the students take questions from their web and sort them into categories using a T-chart to help.

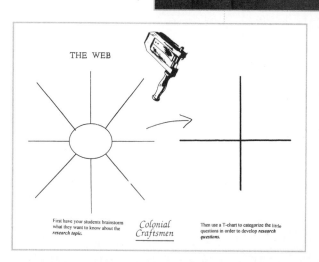

THE WEB

First have your students brainstorm what they want to know about the *research topic*.

Colonial Craftsmen

Then use a T-chart to categorize the *little questions* in order to develop *research questions*.

5. After a few sentence strips are placed on the chart, Kate asks if anyone sees a pattern developing. Why are the questions being placed on the board the way they are? At first the only pattern students notice is that all the sentence strips of the same color are being grouped together. Kate responds to this observation by saying, "That's right, but why are the questions on the same-colored strips?"

6. She continues this process until all the sentences have been shared and placed and the students have discovered the pattern—that like questions go together.

7. Finally, students generate the big questions for the research project by stating in their own words what the categories are.

Below are examples of completed T-charts. When creating these T-charts, be sure to keep the language in "kid speak" to make the charts meaningful to students (*What kind of tools and work area does a colonial cabinetmaker need?*). But also use proper terminology (*capital resources*) to reinforce the concept you are teaching. The following charts depict what the students actually said and what the technical terminology for the broad concepts were.

Colonial Craftsmen

Cabinetmaker

★ What kind of tools or workshop do colonial cabinetmakers need?
  • What tools do they use?
  • Where do they get their tools?
  • What kind of shop do they need?

★ What materials do they need for their work?
  • Do they use water or fire to make cabinets?
  • Do they use wood?
  • What kind of wood do cabinet makers use?
  • Where do they get their supplies?

★ Who are the people that work with the cabinet maker?
  • How many workers do you need?
  • How many apprentices in a shop?
  • Who teaches the cabinet maker his craft?
  • Are there any women cabinetmakers?

★ What do cabinet makers make?
  • Do cabinet makers make furniture besides cabinets?
  • How do they deliver what they have made to their customers?
  • Do cabinet makers build houses?

★ "BIG" Questions
• "little" Questions

Colonial Craftsmen

Cabinetmaker

★ What kind of tools or workshop do colonial cabinet makers need?
  • What ___s do they u___?
  • ___ do they get ___ir tools?
  • What kind of shop do they need?

Capital Resources

★ What materials do they need for their w___k?
  • Do they use ___r or fire to ma___ ___abinets
  • Do they ___ wood?
  • What ___d of wood do ___inet makers use?
  • Where do they get their supplies?

Natural Resources

★ Who are the people that work with the cabinet maker?
  • How man___ ___rkers do you ___d?
  • How ___y apprentices in ___ shop?
  • ___o teaches the cabinet maker his craft?
  • Are there any women cabinetmakers?

Human Resources

★ What do cabinet makers make?
  • Do cabinet mak___s make furnitu___ ___esides cabinets?
  • How do t___ ___ deliver what t___ have made to ___ customers?
  • D___ ___inet makers build houses?

Products and Services

★ "BIG" Questions
• "little" Questions

Now the students are closer to beginning their research. They have formulated the big questions on which they need to concentrate. Finding the answers to the little questions will answer students' big question as well. You can help your students see how little and big questions fit together by having them further organize their questions on a jellyfish, as shown at right. This graphic organizer will help direct their search and serve as a visual reminder to them of where they are going and how the pieces of a report fit together. What are my big questions? What little questions will help me answer my big questions?

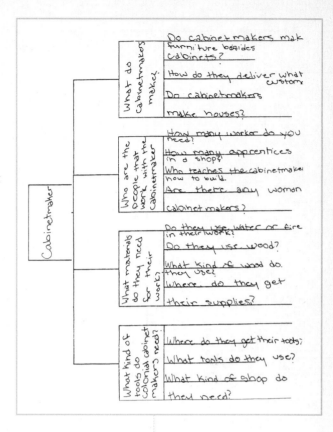

Modifying Questions

As we noted in Chapter 1, the research process is not linear. At any time researchers may need to modify what they have already done. By revisiting the steps along the way, students can fine-tune anything that needs to be changed or adjusted.

Students often have to revise questions to discover the answers they are seeking. The scaffolding built in for students, such as the webs and jellyfish organizers, are meant to provide support through structure. They are not, however, intended to lock students into a course that isn't headed anywhere. Students may revise at any time.

Sometimes a question simply needs to be reworded. For example, "Do colonial candle-makers use wax to make candles?" may need to be changed to "What materials do colonial candle-makers use to make candles?" Other times, as your students learn more about a topic, they realize that other questions are more informative. For example, "Where do colonial candle-makers get the supplies they need to make candles?"

Name _____ Date _____

Using Student Reflections to Plan Mini-Lessons

As discussed in Chapter 2, students write a daily Reflections Log after each research/writing period. The examples below show a problem two students were continuing to have with formulating good questions. These Reflections generated the following mini-lesson, in which assessing questions was once again discussed.

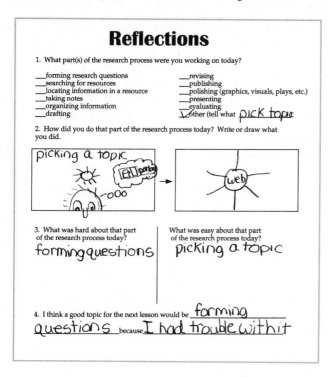

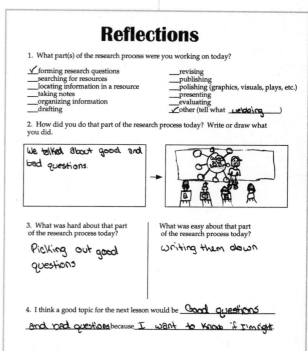

Identifying Good Research Questions

PURPOSE

To reteach students who are still having difficulty moving from little questions to big questions.

MATERIALS

- charts and questions from original activity
- overhead projector
- transparencies from student Reflections Logs

BEFORE THE MINI-LESSON

Read over the students' Reflections Logs to determine who is having a problem with questioning. Compile a list of students who will be included in your mini-lesson.

Kate begins the research period by talking about the previous day's research and what her students will be doing today in class. Most students will be moving on to the "gathering information" stage of the process. However, Kate has noticed that some students still aren't comfortable with questioning.

After announcing, "Today's mini-lesson is brought to you by Caitlyn and Jason!" she shares their Reflections Logs with the whole class. She reads the names of several students who had similar difficulties and then invites them to a mini-lesson where questioning strategies will be discussed and clarified. She also invites anyone else in the class who wants a review to join the group.

PRESENTING THE LESSON

While the rest of the class works independently, Kate meets with the small group. They review how little questions turn into big questions. Using a transparency of a T-chart, Kate reviews how to take little questions and group them into categories of similar questions. She revisits the questions the class had categorized in the earlier lesson, and asks each student to look at his or her original web (see page 41) and decide which questions might go in each category. In this small-group setting, the students ask very specific questions about what they didn't understand and receive immediate feedback from Kate. Once they feel comfortable with questioning, they are free to leave the small group and work on gathering information.

By using student feedback, Kate is able to assess individual needs and enable all students to work at their own pace and competency level.

Only a few of Kate's students needed more direct instruction on developing research questions. She meets with them in a small group while other students continue to work independently.

As you can see, what students record in their REFLECTIONS LOGS guides daily instruction. You plan mini-lessons based on what they tell you they need to know or have found difficult. Instruction is meaningful for students because it is generated by them to help them with the stumbling blocks they encounter when applying research skills during an authentic task (as opposed to a worksheet from a research "how-to" book). Reflections logs also help students develop metacognition about their own skills, an important step toward independence.

Asking the Right Questions

Students gradually become aware that not all questions are necessarily appropriate for a research project and learn to develop questions that are just right. If a question is too narrow (for example, "Do killer whales eat people?"), then once the specific answer to the question is found, you are through. Yes/no questions or questions that have one-word answers are not broad enough for a report.

If questions are too large, however, you run into problems as well. For example, "What gods or spirits do Native Americans worship?" needs to be narrowed down to a particular group (East Woodland, Plains, etc.) or tribe, so the question would be, "What gods or spirits do the Plains Indians worship?" Otherwise, students will be overwhelmed by the research task.

As you present mini-lessons and work with small groups and individual students, encourage students to classify their questions as "big" or "little" and think about whether the questions are appropriate for their research task. One useful mini-lesson is to take students' own questions, copy them on an overhead, and think aloud about whether the questions are researchable. Talk about what makes a good research question, using the terminology "big and little questions" to reinforce the idea of categorizing little questions to develop the big, researchable ones. You can repeat this mini-lesson as needed, using a variety of topics and questions, to help students internalize the process of breaking down and evaluating their questions. Asking the right questions is a difficult skill; repeated modeling and practice gives students the experience they need to do it on their own.

Where to Next?

Now that your students have formulated good research questions, you are ready to move on to the next step in the AGOP process, *gathering information*. In Chapter 4 you will see how to use the student Reflections Logs to guide instruction and develop strategies for students to be successful in gathering information.

Gathering Information

Once students have formulated their research questions as described in Chapter 3, they are ready to focus on the *G* in AGOP, *gathering information*. In today's information-centered world, the number of resources and ideas related to a topic may seem endless. However, it is important to keep in mind that your students are searching specifically for answers to the questions they've generated. In this chapter, we will show you ways to help your students successfully develop the skills they need to select resources and to locate the information within those resources.

Where to Begin

A good place to begin is by determining which general skills you hope your students will develop during this phase of the process. You might set some of the following outcomes as your goals for students:

- Identifying appropriate sources
- Selecting information appropriate to the task
- Accessing information efficiently
- Gathering accurate information that's relevant to the subject
- Recording information efficiently
- Citing sources properly

Keep in mind that the ultimate goal for your students is independence!

Assessing Students' Information-Gathering Skills

To determine how well your students gather information, it's not necessary to step outside your current research project. To assess their individual skill levels, simply take a close look at the resources they select when they try to locate information. Are they on the right track? Do they use a variety of resources?

For example, when Kate's school installed an encyclopedia on the computer in the media center, Kate found her students were attracted by the new technology. But it wasn't a good resource for their current topic, specific counties in the state of Maryland. Students were anxious to get their hands on the computer; they all lined up and spent most of the research period waiting to use the device, even when one student after another came away empty-handed from their search. *Calvert County? Kent? Garrett?* The outcome was always the same…NO INFORMATION. The questions the students were asking were just too narrow for an encyclopedia, even an encyclopedia on a CD-ROM!

Kate's observations were validated by the Reflections Logs her students wrote after those sessions. After the computer experience, for example, Kate discovered that the consensus seemed to be that you shouldn't waste your time standing in line for the computer. After such a negative experience, students were very receptive to subsequent mini-lessons on what various resources contain, how they are organized, and what they are appropriate for.

The following is an example of a lesson Kate uses with her students before they begin researching colonial craftsmen. Like Kate's lesson, your instruction should relate directly to your current research project, and to the problems your students are encountering. Here Kate guides students to locate the best resources for their topic by helping them determine the right places to look.

Mining the Media Center for the "Mother Lode" of Information

PURPOSE

To help students efficiently locate information by selecting appropriate resources.

MATERIALS

- chart listing colonial craftsmen
- index cards
- markers
- chart paper
- research folders (where students keep their graphic organizers, notes, drafts, etc., during the research project)

- media center
- computers (for Internet access and CD-ROM applications)
- encyclopedias
- trade books (nonfiction)
- timer

Students create a chart listing the resources they know about in the school's media center.

BEFORE THE MINI-LESSON

Kate arranged for time in the media center. While still in the classroom, she had her students examine the questions they had posed about their chosen craftsmen to help them decide where to begin to look for facts. They brainstormed and listed on chart paper all the places in the media center they could search for the information they needed. She used this list of resources to make index cards for the mini-lesson. She wrote the name of one resource on each card. For example, she wrote "Internet" on one card and "Encyclopedia" on another.

Each group receives an index card indicating the resource they are to explore.

PRESENTING THE LESSON

Kate allows her students to work in like-interest groups. Like-interest groups consist of students researching the same craftsman. She gives each group an index card with a resource written on it. Her directions then are very simple!

Kate: We are going to work in the media center this morning. I have given each of your groups an index card with the resource you will be using to search for information. When we get there, I am going to set the timer for 30 minutes. That's all the time you get today to gather facts. As you work today, I want you to find as much information as you can on your questions. But I also want you to evaluate the resource you use. Is the resource you are assigned to use good for finding the answers you are seeking? Be prepared at the end of this session to explain to your classmates why the resource is or is not a useful resource.

▲ Students hunt for information on their research topics in multiple sources.

After the session, back in the classroom, Kate leads her class in a collective share to discuss the initial search in the media center. She records on the chalkboard the successes or frustrations they experienced during their searches.

Kate's students give the materials they used varied reviews during the collective share. Some materials get very high ratings, such as the trade book series about colonial craftsmen, while others are deemed "terrible." Based on their discussion, Kate's students begin to realize that if the topic is very specific, such as colonial craftsmen, some resources, like the encyclopedia, are not helpful. Even sites on the Internet may produce no useful information because the topic is too narrow in its focus. She concludes her lesson with a question: "Does the nature of the topic itself dictate where you should look for information?"

The students then fill out their Reflections Logs. They include comments such as these:

🌀 "Don't bother to use the computer for this. It stinks!"

🌀 "The encyclopedia is a big waste of time!"

🌀 "You should use the books with the old-time pictures on them. They're really good!"

Many of the students ask in their logs for more instruction on picking resources. Therefore, the next research session begins with a review of the previous session. Kate and her students review and refine information-gathering strategies. Then the students compile a list of "appropriate" resources for this topic. As you can see, the students' Reflections Logs are already giving the mini-lessons their direction.

Friends in the Right Places

Your school media specialist should be a valuable resource to your students, helping them to discover all the wonderful materials available in the media center. Your media specialist is also the key to procuring resources your school does not already own. He or she can be invaluable for scheduling speakers or ordering books, periodicals, and other resources to support your program. Most media specialists look to the classroom teachers for suggestions when building and strengthening their collections.

In addition, there are many commercial resources available to assist you in directing your students toward materials that will help them locate the information they seek. A publication such as *The New York Public Library Kid's Guide to Research* by Deborah Heiligman (1998, New York: Scholastic) is an excellent resource for you to use to help your students locate and evaluate resources for their reports. It gives practical advice and easy-to-apply strategies for finding and using materials that are the most appropriate for a given topic. Although students' Reflections Logs should drive your selection of the mini-lessons you plan for your class, this book is a handy reference in planning the content for those lessons.

Real Life Makes for the Best Lessons

Whenever possible, use actual examples of whatever has given students difficulty in gathering information. If the index in a resource is difficult to understand, and therefore hard to use, make an overhead of it and discuss the problem with the class. The more authenticity you can bring to your mini-lessons, the more powerful they will be to your students.

One of Kate's students confided to her that she wasn't having much luck with the index in a book she had selected. Although the book itself was a good choice, Megan found herself struggling with it and became very frustrated. The question she was trying to answer was, "What did the Tidewater Indians do for fun?" Kate asked to see the book, and the problem became clear at once. Megan needed to think of a synonym for "fun" in order to use the index efficiently. Megan's dilemma became the topic of the next mini-lesson.

Index Problems: Using the Right Words

PURPOSE

To have students use the strategy of thinking of a synonym for a word if they can't locate it in the index or table of contents.

MATERIALS

🌀 Megan's book (the one she was using as a resource)

🌀 overhead markers

🌀 overhead of the index from Megan's book

🌀 overhead of the table of contents from Megan's book

PRESENTING THE LESSON

Kate explains to the class that Megan had found an excellent resource for her research. When she looked in the index and table of contents, however, she couldn't find out what Tidewater Indians did for fun.

Kate: Take a look at the index from the book Megan used. If you look at all the listings that begin with the letter "F," you can see there is no listing for "fun." Where else could she look for this information?

Aileen: She should pick another book.

Greg: Yeah, if it's not in the index, she shouldn't waste her time.

Kate: But this is a great resource! I don't think Megan should give up so quickly. Perhaps if I read you the whole index you might come up with some other ideas. Listen carefully. [Note that this book had a brief two-page index, not an uncommon length in the intermediate grades. With a lengthy index, an alternative strategy might be to have your students brainstorm synonyms for their target term; a thesaurus could be used as a resource.]

Kate reads the index aloud.

Kate: Algonquin, amusements, Annemessex, appearance....

Marco: Hey, wait a minute! Doesn't "amusements" mean "fun"? Like things you do at an amusement park? Maybe we should look at the heading "amusements" to see if they have any information about what these people liked to do for fun?

Kate picks up Megan's book and opens to the page listed in the index. There, between pages 29 and 31, was great information about how Tidewater Indians had fun! Kate uses an overhead marker to circle the word "amusements."

Kate: Let's see if we can find some other words in this index that might help.

Karen: I see "dancing."

Jon: What about "games"?

Kate: Wonderful! Megan thought this book contained no information about how Tidewater Indians had fun. But, by thinking of other words that might mean the same thing as "fun," we were able to help her find the information she was looking for.

Kate then shares the table of contents on the overhead with the class. She asks them to skim the contents. They quickly spot the listing "Amusements" and realize that this is another way they can locate the facts they want.

Kate finishes the lesson by summing up what her students had discovered. Even though it seemed as though the resource didn't contain any information on the topic Megan wanted, using synonyms had proved to be a great help. Students had learned a lesson: Don't give up too quickly on a resource. Be flexible in your thinking.

The Worst-Case Scenario: A "Bad" Index

During the same Native American project, another student ran into a different problem. Brent was using a book specifically about the Tidewater Indians of Maryland and Virginia. He was researching transportation. He already knew that these tribes traveled by water, so he looked up "boat" in the index. There was nothing listed. He then looked under "C" for "canoe." Still no luck! As you can see in the index to the right, the information he was looking for was listed under "I" for "Indian boats"!

Kate began the next research session with a mini-lesson "brought to you by Brent!" Kate guided her class through a discussion on why this index was poorly written. What had made it so difficult for Brent to locate information on boats? The problem turned out to be the modifier "Indian," which had been placed before boat in the index. The students concluded that a book about Indians shouldn't list any information under "Indian" anything! "Indian boats" should be listed under "B," "Indian clothing" under "C," "Indian hairstyles" under "H," etc. Once again they discussed the need to be flexible and to think of alternative ways to access information in obviously good resources. Books aren't always perfect.

I

Indian boats, 69-73.

Indian clothing, 17, 22, 26, 39, 42-43, 98, 121.

Indian hair styles, 97-99.

Indian health, 96.

Indian houses, 2-10, 26, 80, 118.

Indian law, 105-107, 109, 111.

Indian money, 85.

Indian religion, 66, 108.

Indian warfare, 45, 52, 61-62, 65, 67-68, 76, 78, 89-91, 93, 100, 103, 127; see also the Powhatan Confederacy.

Iroquois, v, vi, 49, 58-60, 68, 69, 83, 88, 90, 93.

Source: Thelma Rushkin (1986). *Indians of the Tidewater Country of Maryland, Virginia, Delaware, and North Carolina.* Lanham, MD: Maryland Historical Press.

Gathering Information from the Internet

Technology has come a long way since the introduction of computers to the classroom. Excellent web sites and search engines specifically designed for intermediate students are now accessible even to novice researchers. These sites didn't even exist five years ago. Search engines, such as <u>Yahooligans</u> **http://www.yahooligans.com/** or <u>Ask Jeeves for Kids</u>, **http://www.ajkids.com/**, are tailor-made to help students access sites designed to provide young researchers with information. These sites are about topics that are of high interest to young readers and are written at a reading level that allows them to understand the information once they have located it. Search engines have become very user-friendly and the list of child-oriented locations on the Internet grows daily.

Students use the Internet to search for information. Their search is guided by a list of teacher-selected sites that are relevant to their topic.

The following is an example of how resources on the World Wide Web can enhance your students' research. Surfing the Internet for needed facts can be fun, but it can also be time-consuming and frustrating, especially for a novice. To solve this problem, you can locate good web sites for your students. Once they learn how to navigate web sites, you can teach them how to locate good sites on their own.

Fourth-grade teacher Jessica Gibson located Internet sites for her students to use as they conducted research on Kenya. She organized these sites on a computer disk. When she wants her students to use these resources, she inserts the disk into a computer that is hooked up to the Internet. Her students then open the "home page" she has stored on her disk. They encounter an attractive page with the following message:

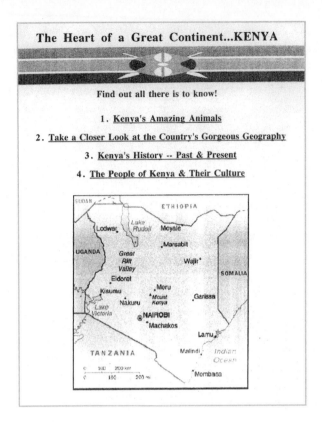

The Heart of a Great Continent...KENYA

Find out all there is to know!

1. Kenya's Amazing Animals

2. Take a Closer Look at the Country's Gorgeous Geography

3. Kenya's History -- Past & Present

4. The People of Kenya & Their Culture

When Jessica's students click on a menu item, they find a collection of web sites on that topic. For example, when students click on Kenya's Amazing Animals, they encounter another attractive screen like this one.

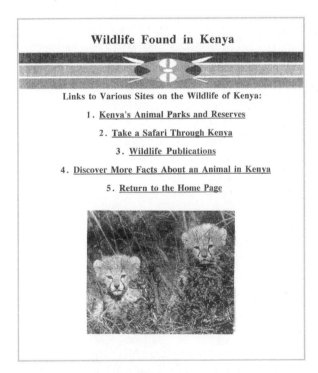

Wildlife Found in Kenya

Links to Various Sites on the Wildlife of Kenya:

1. Kenya's Animal Parks and Reserves

2. Take a Safari Through Kenya

3. Wildlife Publications

4. Discover More Facts About an Animal in Kenya

5. Return to the Home Page

They can then click to visit a web site for each topic. Or, they can return to the first screen and select a collection of web sites on other information about Kenya.

Internet Resources

<>FREE (Federal Resources for Educational Excellence) web site **http://www.ed.gov/free/** has links to hundreds of learning resources. Once you are at the FREE web site, you can click on resources for students. Or you can go directly to **http://www.ed.gov/free/ kids.html** for student links. Your students can select links to the National Aeronautics and Space Administration's StarChild: A Learning Center for Young Astronomers **http://starchild.gsfc.nasa. gov/docs/StarChild/ StarChild.html** and to the Peace Corps Kids World **http://www.peacecorps. gov/kids/index.html**, or they can select scores of student resources from government agencies including the White House, Environmental Protection Agency, Department of Treasury, FBI, National Science Foundation, and the Centers for Disease Control and Prevention.

Time Management Tips

Searching the Internet is an important skill for your students to develop, but it is difficult to do with every project because it can be very time-consuming. Kate usually walks her students through the Internet search process with at least one research project a year. It's important that they see how they can use search engines to locate sites, search sites for information, and bookmark sites with pertinent information. Recently her class was researching Chincoteague ponies. (They were reading *Misty of Chincoteague* by Marguerite Henry and were working on a mini-report to go along with the novel.) Together with her students, she discovered a *Misty* web site. They checked out all the information it contained but only bookmarked the pages with information they needed for their assignment. They came away with two valuable products: the search experience and a disk of sites they could use over and over again.

More Management Tips

What if you have no time or talent to create your own collection of Internet resources? You can have your technology-savvy parent volunteers or high school volunteers locate kid-friendly sites for you. They can create disks with home pages for you like Jessica Gibson did for her students. Or, your

Students use sticky-notes to mark information they want to have copied from Kate's vertical file.

volunteers can simply bookmark the web addresses for particular topics. You can store these bookmarks on a disk for use in future years. Volunteers can check these sites every year to keep your resources current.

To help students use information gathered on line, Kate created a vertical file of printed sites because many students had a difficult time reading the information on the monitor. At first, she allowed them to print out the information they had accessed. However, this proved to be another time-consuming task. To save time Kate printed out good resources and filed them. Her students could look through these resources and ask for copies of the materials in the vertical file by using a sticky-note to make a request. Her students found using the hard copy very useful in the information-gathering process. Many of the students used highlighters (matching the color codes they were using for their project) to mark the chunks of information they were seeking. It worked well!

Evaluating Sources

Your students will need to evaluate the sources they use for gathering information to determine if the sources are reliable and useful. Together you and your students can decide what makes a good source. Thinking about how current a source is, who wrote or compiled it, and how the information is organized and presented can help students determine the value of a source. In making their judgments, your students may find forms such as the ones on the following pages helpful.

A good source to help you get started on the Internet is Don and Debbie Leu's book *Teaching with the Internet: Lessons from the Classroom* (Norwood, MA: Christopher-Gordon, 2000).

Also check out *Getting Started With the Internet* by Peter Levy (Scholastic, 2000).

Name _____ Date _____

☆ ☆ Nonfiction Book ☆ ☆ ☆

Title of the Book _____

Author _____

(1) Is the author an expert on the subject? ☐ Yes ☐ No ☐ Unsure

(2) On the back of the title page check for the following information:

   ◎ Copyright date _____

   ◎ Number of editions _____

(3) Is the copyright date recent enough to include the newest facts on the topic?

   ☐ Yes ☐ No ☐ Unsure

(4) Are there pictures and diagrams? ☐ Yes ☐ No

   Are they helpful? ☐ Yes ☐ No

(5) Is the book convenient to use? Rate the following:

   ◎ Index: ☐ Excellent ☐ Fair ☐ Not helpful

   ◎ Table of Contents: ☐ Excellent ☐ Fair ☐ Not helpful

   ◎ Headings: ☐ Excellent ☐ Fair ☐ Not helpful

   ◎ Vocabulary in Italics: ☐ Excellent ☐ Fair ☐ Not helpful

(6) Does the book cover the topic fully and is the information easy to understand?

   Why or why not? _____

   _____

(7) What made you select this book as a resource? ☐ Graphic on Cover ☐ Title

(8) What overall rating would you give this resource?

   ☐ Use with caution ☐ Good basic information ☐ Excellent for assignment

Name _____   Date _____

Web Site

Web Site Address   http:// _____

Title of Web Site _____

Who wrote this (author, editor, institution)?

_____

Content:

◎ Does this site provide text only?   ☐ Yes   ☐ No

◎ Does this site provide text with graphics?   ☐ Yes   ☐ No

◎ Does this site include a multimedia presentation along with the text?

☐ Yes   ☐ No

◎ Do these graphics and/or multimedia contribute to the topic?   ☐ Yes   ☐ No

◎ What is the point of view of the site?

☐ Inform   ☐ Persuade   ☐ Fact   ☐ Opinion

Currency:

◎ When was this site written or last updated?

_____

Rate this web site:

☐ Use with caution   ☐ Good basic information   ☐ Excellent for assignment

Be Sure Students Have Access to Needed Resources

ust as frustrating as a topic that's too broad is one about which a student can't locate enough information. Never allow students to research a topic that is unresearchable within the materials available in your classroom or school library. If a student runs into this dilemma, help broaden the topic, as Kate did in the following example.

One of Kate's students had her heart set on researching the Pacific white-sided dolphin. After two or three very frustrating sessions trying to locate information on this particular species, Kate helped her broaden her search by changing the topic to dolphins in general. While there was only minimal information to be had on the Pacific white-sided dolphin in the school media center, this information was easily incorporated into a broader report on dolphins. Sometimes a topic is just too obscure for novice researchers, and we need to help students broaden their search.

Taking Notes

e have already shown in Chapter 3 how students can organize their "little research questions" into "big questions." As students take notes, their little questions get answered. After answering all their little questions, they have plenty of information to answer their big questions and plenty of information to include in their reports. In Chapter 3 we used one color to color-code all the little questions that contributed to answering each big question about students' topics. We suggest you have

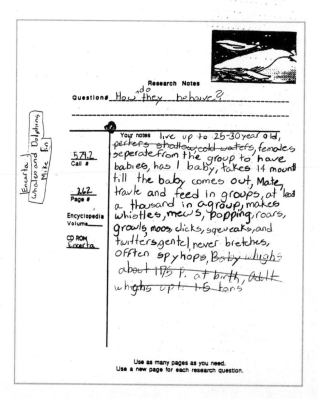

students continue to color-code as they proceed in the research process because it will help them to keep the information they gather organized. On the note page shown on page 64, the student has used a marker to draw a color code on his notes.

Students can color-code their notes several ways. Kate likes to photocopy note-taking sheets on colored paper. Or, you can have your class mark the corners of their papers with colored markers. Students also like to use colored stickers (plain colored stickers used for filing or marking items at yard sales work well) to color-code their notes.

Picking the Format

Whether you have your students use note cards or a note-taking sheet similar to the one shown on the previous page is entirely up to you. It is easier for intermediate students, particularly younger students, to manage the information if it is written on a note-taking sheet. If you decide that your students are mature enough to use note cards, the color-coding principle remains the same. For cards, either use colored cards or have the students mark the cards with the color that corresponds to the big question to which they pertain. Write the question on the first card. All information pertaining to that question will go into that stack of cards. (Use rubber bands or you'll end up with cards all over the place.) Similarly, for note-taking sheets, have students code with the same color all the sheets that are relevant to the same big question.

Citing Sources

Whether they use cards or sheets, students need to note where they found their information. In the sample on page 64, you can see that the student has recorded his source on the left side of the paper; he wrote down the title, author, publisher, and publication year. He has included the page number, and because this source was a library book, he also has included the call number. This type of information will help in two ways. First, if students need to return to a specific resource for clarification, it will be easy to do. Second, when the report is completed and students need to compile a bibliography, all the information will be right there for them.

Note-Taking: Using Their Own Words

Regardless of the note-taking format you choose for your students, be sure to emphasize gathering "chunks" of information. Never allow students to copy complete passages or even sentences when recording the information they have found. They should copy only key words or phrases in order to compile fragment notes on the topic. The following mini-lesson illustrates how to model this skill for students.

Fragment Notes— No Sentences, Please!

PURPOSE

To have students gather information by writing chunks of information from their resources.

MATERIALS

🌀 transparency of a passage from the book *The Printers*, written and illustrated by Leonard Everett Fisher as part of the Colonial American Craftsmen Series, 1965, New York: Franklin Watts, p. 34.

🌀 transparency of note-taking sheet

🌀 transparency markers

BEFORE THE MINI-LESSON

Kate presented the following passage on an overhead projector and read it aloud to her class.

"The early printing presses were wooden machines that stood a foot or two taller than a man. Running through the upright supports was a waist-high, tablelike frame called a *carriage*. On the carriage was a wooden plank that slid back and forth along two rails. Fastened on top of the plank was another frame called a *coffin*."

PRESENTING THE LESSON

Kate: Today's lesson is going to focus on taking notes in your own words. Remember, you cannot copy whole sections from the book. That would be *plagiarism*, and that is against the law.

You must write everything in your own words, but you may use "chunks" (a word or a phrase) of the information you find. When taking notes, copy only key words or big ideas. We are going to practice today using the passage I have just read to you. First, let's look at each sentence and underline important facts we need for our reports.

The students make the following suggestions for facts they want underlined:

> "The early printing presses were <u>wooden machines</u> that stood a <u>foot or two taller than a man</u>. Running through the <u>upright supports</u> was a <u>waist-high, tablelike frame called a carriage</u>. On the carriage was a wooden plank that slid back and forth along two rails. Fastened on top of the plank was another <u>frame called a coffin</u>."

Kate: Now let's write these facts on the note-taking sheet. For the question, I am going to write the following: *Early Printing Presses: What did they look like? What were they made of?* In the "Your notes" section, tell me some facts I could write from this passage.

Robb: They're made of wood, so I'd write that down.

Kate: Good point. What else?

Maria: The height is important. The passage says the presses were one or two feet taller than a man.

Javier: Yeah, and there were the two frames. The carriage was waist high.

Maria: The coffin was the other frame; it was fastened to a movable plank on top.

Kate records the class's suggestions on the overhead:

- made of wood
- foot or two taller than a man
- two frames
- carriage—about waist high
- coffin—fastened to a movable plank on top of the carriage

Kate: Nice work. We've written notes that capture the main idea in the paragraph, and we've only used key words; we didn't copy any sentences. Later, when we decide to use these facts in a paragraph, it will be easy to put them in our own words. We call these notes fragment notes, and that's how you'll take notes for your research.

These examples show how students wrote their information in chunks.

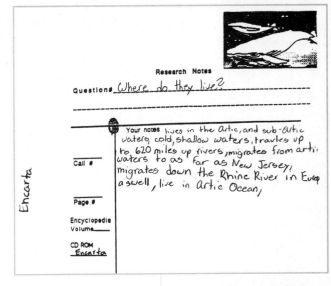

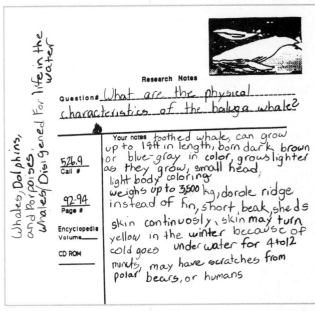

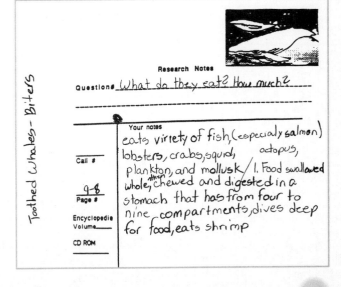

Taking Notes From Videos or Movies

Don't overlook the fact that videotapes and movies can be an extremely valuable resource when it comes to gathering information for reports. For some of your students, particularly students who are visual learners or who aren't proficient readers, it may be the best method. But, special note-taking techniques are needed for nonprint material. One simple method we have used is called "skinny notes." ("Skinny notes" is Ruth Garner's version of note-taking of the type suggested by Wayne Otto.) The following mini-lesson describes how Kate used this method in her classroom when having her students work on a project researching rocks and minerals.

M I N I - L E S S O N

Finding Facts in Films

PURPOSE

To help students learn techniques for taking notes from a video or film.

MATERIALS

❋ *Rocks and Minerals* (a 15-minute video about the special characteristics of rocks and minerals)

❋ transparency of "skinny notes"

❋ transparency markers

PRESENTING THE LESSON

Kate: Today we will be watching a video titled *Rocks and Minerals.* It contains lots of good information that you could include in your reports. But we do have one small problem we need to talk about, and that is, how do you take notes when watching a video?

Kendra: Yeah, you'd have to write real fast to get everything down from a video.

Tom: Maybe we could work with a partner. That way you could take turns writing the facts down, so you wouldn't have to go so fast.

Reiko: You can always pause the tape to write notes, and you can rewind to hear something you missed.

Kate: Those are all great strategies, and maybe we can use some of your suggestions. I am going to model a method for you today to show you an easier way to go about your note-taking. [She turns on the overhead showing the "skinny notes" format. See sample below.] It's called "skinny notes." Can anyone tell me why?

Keith: Because you write the notes in skinny columns.

Kate: That's right! But there is a little more you need to know before we begin. We will be watching the video three times this morning. The first time through, we are going to focus on the main topic the film is trying to tell us about. The second time we watch, we're going to see if we can figure out the big questions the filmmaker had in mind when making this video. We will write these main ideas or key words in the first column.

The third time we watch, we'll put any important details that go with the key words in the center column. We'll be writing these details beside the main idea it supports.

Finally, we'll use the third column to summarize the information we learned from the video.

Now Kate shows the video and models the steps described above. She draws students into the process by thinking aloud and asking for their input and advice.

The next time she uses this strategy with her class, she will review the procedure and only use direct instruction if the need for it arises. Also, if some students aren't confident about trying the strategy themselves, she will work with them individually or in small groups.

As your students use "skinny notes," be sure to have them record information about the name of the video at the top of their notes so that it will be easy for them to cite the source in their bibliography. In the example at right, the student has recorded the video title, *Rocks and Minerals*.

Video/Film Notes

Title Rocks + Minerals   Date 2-5-98

Key Words	Running Notes	Summary
Minerals	physical properties,	These are different physical properties of rocks and minerals. We use these to identify rocks and minerals.
Colors	different colors	
Streak	Minerals make different streaks	
Luster	glassy, dulle, shinny,	
Hardness	scratch tests	
Density	amount taken up, how heavy it is	
Cleavage	how it breaks	
Fracture	eregular breaking	
Igniouis	magma pushed up and hardens into rock	
Sedeminrty	different rocks cemented together	
Metamorphic	rocks under heat and pressure change into different rocks	

Moving Right Along

Once your students have had adequate time and opportunity to gather the information they need for their research questions, it is time to move on to the next phase of the AGOP process: organizing and writing about the information they have found. Chapter 5 explains how you can help your students organize what they have learned.

Organizing and Writing

After students have gathered information from a variety of sources, it's time to organize the information for writing a report. In this chapter, we focus on the *O* in AGOP—*organizing and writing*. Organizing and writing include the students' preparation for writing the report as well as their drafting, revising, editing, and proofreading of the report.

Where Are We So Far?

The graphic organizers on this page and the next give you an overview of where we are in the research process and how this chapter fits in. First, the web and jellyfish graphic organizers illustrate how your students moved from generating research questions to organizing them into big questions in Chapter 3. The next chart summarizes Chapter 4, showing how students gather information related to their questions. In this chapter we continue the process, by showing you how to take your students from their notes to a fragment outline, and then from the fragment outline to paragraphs (see graphic organizers on the top of page 72). Once students complete paragraph graphics, they are ready to write their rough drafts. At this point, the paragraphs they have written can be revised, edited, proofread, and used in the final drafts of students' reports. We provide the details for the organizing and writing step in the rest of this chapter.

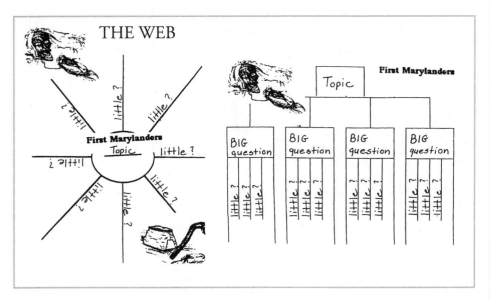

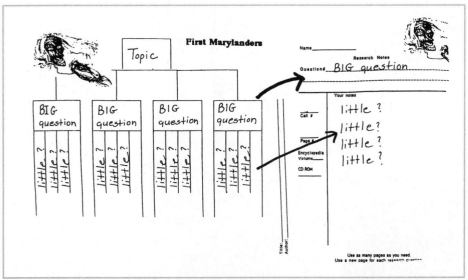

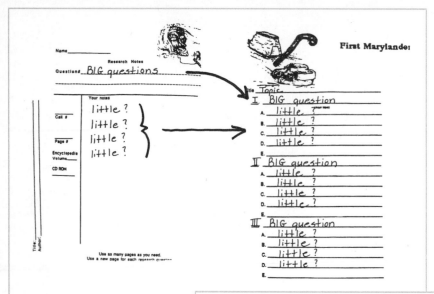

Kate usually exhibits a poster showing these graphic organizers. This enables her students to visualize where they are in the process and helps them stay organized and focused. Pictured below is the poster of organizers she uses during a research project on whales. Students can refer to it at any time to see what steps they have completed and what steps they need to take next.

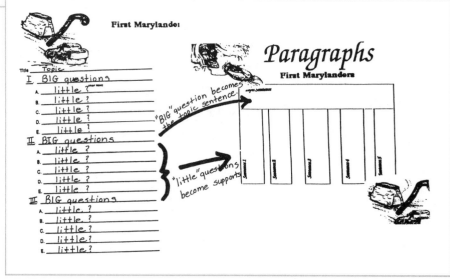

Students consult a poster of a project's graphic organizers to monitor their progress during research.

Organizing Notes

In Chapter 4 we showed how students color-coded their notes to keep straight all the information relevant to each of their big questions. Now you will see how the color-coding technique is continued in the next stage of the process. Your students are now ready to proceed by organizing the information they have gathered into an outline. The following mini-lesson illustrates how to go about teaching this skill to your students. We use a project on whales as an example.

M I N I - L E S S O N

Discovering Outlines

PURPOSE

To help students learn to organize information into an outline.

MATERIALS

♻ colored sentence strips to match color code
  (or plain sentence strips and colored markers)

♻ black markers

♻ masking tape or tacks

♻ large bulletin board or chalkboard

♻ graphic organizer of whale report outline

♻ student research folder (containing the notes they have taken)

♻ colored stickers (plain colored stickers used for filing work well)

BEFORE THE MINI-LESSON

Select a group of researchers that has completed gathering the information about their whale. Since they have worked as a team during the gathering stage of the process, the information they have collected should be the same. Make a sentence strip showing the name of the whale the group has researched (the title of the report) and a different-colored sentence strip for each of the big questions (main topics) the students researched. For whales that would include:

♻ Where whales live   ♻ What whales eat

♻ How whales behave   ♻ What whales look like

Now give the group you've selected the colored sentence strips. Ask them to write the information they have found on the sentence strips. Remind them to match the color of the sentence strip on which the fact is written to that of the big question it answers. Instruct them to use their best handwriting and to record only one fact on each strip. Ask them to copy it exactly as they have it in their notes and to begin each fact with a capital letter. (Capital letters are used to conform with conventions for fragment outlines in English books.) However, the *No sentences, please!* rule is still in effect at this point. Now you are ready for the lesson!

PRESENTING THE LESSON

Kate has taped the title of the report to the center of the chalkboard. She also has taped to the board the four colored strips on which she had written the main topics.

Kate: Most of you are at the point in your research where you have gathered all the information needed for your reports. But before you begin your rough drafts, there's one more prewriting step you can take to make the actual writing easier. You are going to organize your facts into an outline.

I have asked the group researching humpback whales to share the facts they have found so you can see how it's done.

Kate invites the group to bring up the sentence strips and tape them to the board. Kate makes sure the students indent the fact strips as they place them on the board, so that the visual representation looks like an outline.

When all the sentence strips are in place, Kate asks the following question of her class:

Kate: What do you notice about how we placed the sentence strips?

Reiko: All the strips that are the same color are together.

Justin: Yeah, and the strips with the facts on them go in a little under the big question.

Kate: Good observations. All the facts that relate to the same big question are together, and the facts are indented under their big question. What else do you notice?

Luis: All the facts start with a capital letter.

Andrea: Yeah, but they're not sentences. The information is still in chunks.

Kate: That's right. Let's take a look at this section of our outline. [Kate points to the section under the heading "What whales eat."] You'll see there are five sentence strips here, five facts about what whales eat. If you read them, you'll notice that two facts are about the whale's diet and three facts are about how the whales get their food. I'm going to rearrange the strips so that the two facts about diet are together, and those about how whales get their food are together. [Kate rearranges the strips.]

Kate: It's so easy at this point to rearrange your facts so that they go together and make better sense. Now when this group goes to write these facts in paragraph form, the facts will flow and they will be very clear to your audience. That's why we make an outline. It helps us see what information we have and how we can best arrange it for our reports.

Finally, Kate uses chalk to fill in what's missing from this outline. She writes in a Roman numeral before each main topic, explaining that this is how main topics are noted on an outline. Then she writes a capital letter before each of the subtopics. She points out that each Roman numeral and capital letter is followed by a period.

She refers her class to the shell outline she has provided for this research project. She asks them to write in the title of their report and each of their main topics. She provides them with stickers to color-code each section of the outline, so that the questions, notes, and outline all match. The box on the next page shows how a completed student outline should look.

An outline highlights the essential information students want to include in their final product and helps students organize that information. Modeling for students how to use an outline enables them to determine the sequence of their report. It is important for students to learn that they must decide which information is most important for their readers to know at the beginning of the report, and to think about ways to make the report flow from section to section. Mini-lessons such as this one can be repeated for different topics until students become comfortable with the skill of outlining.

I. ___The Beluga Whale___
   (main topic)
   A. ___toothed whale___
   B. ___up to 18ft. in length___
   C. ___bron dark or blue-gray___
   D. ___weighs up to 3,600 kilograms___
   E. ___has dorsle ridge instead of fin___
II. ___How they behave___
   A. ___live up to 25-30 years old___
   B. ___perfers shallow and cold waters___
   C. ___females se.perate from group to have babies___
   D. ___takes 14 maonths for a babie to come out.___
   E. ___baby weighs 170 pounds at birth___
III. ___where they live___
   A. ___they live in the artic, and sub-artic___
   B. ___travles up to 620 miles during migration___
   C. ___migrates from artic waters to as far as NJ___
   D. ___migrates down Rhin River in Europe___
   E. ___lives in the artic ocean___

The Information Shuffle

In the process of ordering information into an outline, students may find that they have notes that do not fit under any big question. Here it is essential to confer with students as they work through their notes and try to organize them. Usually students have too much information, and they need assistance in choosing which notes are appropriate. By asking them to provide reasoning for their choice of information (e.g., "What big question does that answer?" or "Why did you choose that detail?"), you can begin helping students to make good choices about selecting information from their notes. On the other hand, students sometimes have too little information.

Kyleen, one of Kate's students, had both problems: too much on one area and too little on another. When Kyleen began working on her outline, she found she had an overabundance of facts about the physical characteristics of the whale she was researching and not enough about its dietary habits.

Kyleen became frustrated when working on her outline because she found she needed more than four lines to write in the facts she had found about the physical characteristics of her whale. At the same time, she had barely enough information to fill in two lines under the heading of "What whales eat." Kyleen wrote about her problem in one of her Reflections Book entries. Kate discussed the problem with her and Kyleen's difficulty became the focus of the next mini-lesson. Here's how it went.

Making Facts Fit

PURPOSE

To help students deal with facts that could fit in more than one place when answering the big questions.

MATERIALS

◆ transparency of Kyleen's notes

◆ transparency of section of outline (two sections only—"What whales eat" and "What whales look like")

◆ transparency markers

PRESENTING THE LESSON

Kate: Today's mini-lesson is brought to you by Kyleen! You see, she ran into a problem when organizing her information into an outline. Some of you have had the same problem with information you are trying to organize. So let's take a look at what you might do.

Kate puts up the first transparency of Kyleen's notes.

Kate: These are the notes Kyleen had trouble organizing on her outline. As you can see, she found a lot of facts about "What whales look like." When she put the facts she had found on her outline, she ran out of room! Does anyone have any suggestions as to what she could do?

Marta: She could write really small so it will all fit.

Kendra: Or, she could just write on another paper and staple it to the outline.

Luis: She could also write in the margins.

Kate: She could do any of those things. Let's try a few things to help Kyleen fit all her information on her outline in a way that will make it easy for her to see how the information she's gathered is related. Watch this! [Kate crosses out the letters in the space where the second heading would go; see sample at right.] What letter comes after E?

Tom: F!

Kate: Right. We'll just continue the letters under the first topic. That way Kyleen knows that all these facts are under this topic.

Title _____

I _____
       (main topic)
   A. _____
   B. _____
   C. _____
   D. _____
   E. _____
   F. _____
   G. _____
   H. _____
   I. _____
   J. _____
   K. _____
II _____
   A. _____
   B. _____
   C. _____
   D. _____
   E. _____

Kate continues to fill in letters until there are enough lines to write in all Kyleen's information.

Kate: As you can see, you don't have to stop at the letter E. You may use as many letters as you need to make your information fit. That would be one way of solving Kyleen's problem. But, if you notice, she still has the problem of not having enough information for "What whales eat." She has only two facts. What could she do?

Kendra: Go back to the library and find more information.

Kyleen: But I've looked everywhere! There isn't any more information.

Kate: Let's look at the information she has found. Here's what she has for the physical characteristics. Could any of the facts she has under this main topic fit under "What whales eat"? Talk in your groups and see if you find anything that we could move.

The class decides that information about the physical characteristics that dictate how a whale obtains and eats food could fit in either category. Whether a whale is "toothed" or "baleen" determines how and what it eats.

Kate puts on a second transparency and, with her students' help, lists any physical traits that influence feeding behavior under "What whales eat." Now Kyleen has balanced her information and has enough to write each of her paragraphs.

Extraneous Information

Even after students have organized their information, they often are left with facts that don't seem to fit any of their big questions, facts that they found and could not resist writing in their notes, even though these facts didn't answer any of the research questions.

Of course your students can leave this extraneous information out of their reports. After all their hard work, however, most students are reluctant to exclude any facts they have managed to unearth. A more satisfying solution is to add a new section to the outline. Kate often has her students create another section labeled, "Other Interesting Facts," where they can share this extra information. This becomes another paragraph in their report.

VI.   Interesting Facts
                               (main topic)
A. Related to Narwhale
B. Names - Sea Canary - White Whale
C. Females live longer than males
D. Beluga - Russian word for "Belii" means white
E. Population - 70,000

Turning Fragment Notes Into Sentences

To help students avoid copying, we emphasize taking fragment notes and using these notes in outlines. But, as they move from outlines to paragraphs, students need to turn their fragment notes into sentences. Some students may have difficulty combining information from their notes into complete sentences. You can help by modeling the thinking required to combine ideas.

For example, one of Kate's students took these notes:

Chesapeake-man-made oyster beds; Chesapeake Bay—rich sources of blue crabs; Motor boats polluting waters.

Kate displayed these notes on an overhead. Then she used think-aloud techniques to help her students see how these facts could be connected.

Kate: Let's see, we have facts here about some of the shellfish that are native to the Chesapeake Bay. Then we have a fact about how too many boats are upsetting the bay's delicate ecosystem. It seems that boating practices on the bay are causing pollution problems that threaten to harm the oyster and blue crab populations. Now, how do these facts relate? How can I combine them into a sentence that makes the best sense of what all this information means?

Kate drew her class into this discussion; together they generated the following examples of how the fragment notes might be combined:

- Oysters and blue crabs in the Chesapeake may be in danger if too many boats pollute the waters.
- When too many boats are in the Chesapeake, the crabs and oysters are endangered.
- Man-made oyster beds and crabs are in danger when boats cause oil or gasoline spills in the Chesapeake.

Once students understand the concept of combining notes, they can work with partners to practice selecting and combining the facts from their notes. Here is a sentence-combining example that students generated from the facts they had in their notes when researching colonial craftsmen.

Notes:
House Building
       Tools—hammers, saws, nails, measure
       Materials—wood, pegs, nails

Combined sentences the students generated:

- Colonial craftsmen used hammers and saws to build their houses. They used the hammer for driving nails into the wood and the saw for cutting wood into the size they wanted.
- Colonial craftsmen needed a hammer and saw to build their houses.
- They used the saws to cut wood to the right size.

From Outline to Paragraphs

After organizing their notes into an outline, your students are now ready to draft their reports. They should write independently to incorporate their own thinking and show their unique voices. For many students, this is the hardest part of the research process. You will need to model how to write one section of the report from the notes relating to one subtopic. For this purpose, students expand and connect ideas. After you model the process, pairs of students can work together to practice expressing ideas in different ways. They can combine answers to little questions and use appropriate connectors and transition words.

To facilitate this part of the process, your students can use a paragraph graphic organizer like the one on page 81. This graphic resembles a table. The topic sentence goes in the tabletop. The supporting sentences go in the table legs. The rule in Kate's class is that there must be at least three supporting sentences for each topic sentence. She has told her class that a table needs at least three legs to stand. The more legs that are added, the sturdier the table will be.

As your students use this paragraph organizer, they will write the information in complete sentences using their own words. Remember, your students started by asking questions. Then they researched those questions. When they moved from their notes to their outline, the questions became a phrase or a heading for the information that would follow. Now the original questions need to be transformed into a statement, an interesting sentence that lets the reader know what will be contained in the paragraph that follows. Students find this the most challenging part of their writing task. Writing good topic sentences is not easy.

The mini-lesson on page 82 is only the beginning of this part of the process and must be continually reinforced through frequent peer or student/teacher conferences.

Sentence 1

Sentence 2

Sentence 3

Sentence 4

Sentence 5

Topic Sentence

Paragraph Organizer

Topic Sentences

PURPOSE

To have students write interesting and varied topic sentences for their paragraphs.

MATERIALS

- chart of the four main research questions
- charts with individual questions written on top line
- markers
- transparency from lesson on outlining (to illustrate that the transition from question to statement has already begun)
- examples of topic sentences written by students

BEFORE THE MINI-LESSON

Prior to this mini-lesson, have your students attempt to write topic sentences for the four main questions they have researched. Collect them and, without using names, read aloud examples of good and bad topic sentences. Ask students which ones they liked and didn't like and why.

The following examples written by Kate's students illustrate topic sentences to avoid. This is what she will read aloud and discuss with the class:

- This paragraph is about where whales live.
- This paragraph is about what whales eat.
- This paragraph is about how whales behave.
- This paragraph is about what whales look like.

Or they might go something like this:

- Where do whales live?
- What do whales eat?
- How do whales behave?
- What do whales look like?

Although these sentences could be used as topic sentences, they are monotonous and uninteresting. They simply won't grab a reader's attention.

Kate posts on the chalkboard the sentences her students have written. She begins by explaining to the class that for the purpose of forming topic sentences for our paragraphs, we now need to revise our big questions. We need to rewrite these original questions as interesting statements or questions that will make the audience want to read our reports. Kate begins with the first big question she has charted.

Kate: Let's begin with the question, "Where do whales live?" If I were turning this question into a statement, I would probably write something like, "Whales can be found in every ocean on the face of the Earth."

Kate writes this sentence on the chart.

Kate: But it really depends on the whale you have selected. Look at the information about where your whale lives. Can you tell me? Talk in your groups and see if you can think of a statement that tells where the whale you researched lives.

The class talks for a few minutes, and then the group that studied beluga whales volunteers the following:

Keith: Beluga whales usually live in the northern Pacific. They live in the ocean itself but migrate to various estuaries during the year.

Kate: That's great! Sounds like a good topic sentence. Do you have facts that explain where and why they migrate as they do?

Sarah: Yes, we do. We have five facts.

Kate: Then it's a great topic sentence. [Writes on chart: *Beluga whales usually live in the northern part of the Pacific Ocean.*]

Kate continues in this manner, having groups offer topic sentences and adding each to the chart. When the chart is complete, she says:

Kate: We now have a topic sentence from each group for the question, "Where do whales live?" You may use one of these topic sentences or write one of your own.

Your students can use a graphic organizer to help them compose paragraphs.

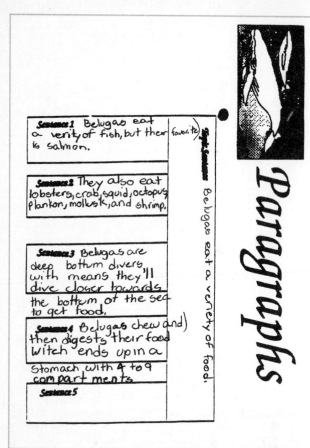

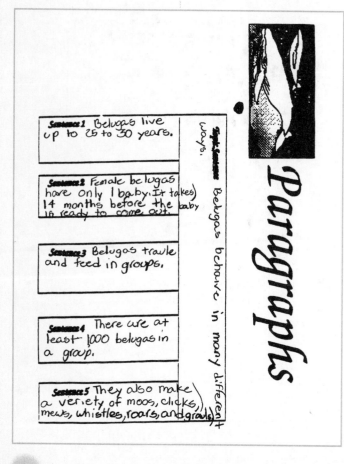

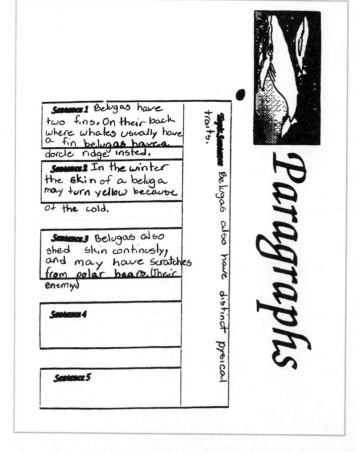

She repeats this same strategy for each of the remaining questions. Now the students are ready to work on paragraphs for each topic sentence graphic. They will use the paragraph graphic as a guide, as illustrated in these examples.

These paragraphs constitute the heart of the report. All the researched information is presented here. But we're not finished yet. In order to showcase the facts your students have found, and give the report a finished, polished look, they need to frame the report with good opening and closing paragraphs. This is the next step in the writing process.

Students use a paragraph graphic organizer to plan each of their supporting paragraphs.

Opening and Closing Paragraphs

Students need to think about their introductory and concluding paragraphs. An important mini-lesson involves helping students think aloud about how they might want to begin and end their reports. Students learn from one another's ideas and enjoy trying to reword their introductions and endings.

The following mini-lesson illustrates just how this is done.

M I N I - L E S S O N

Bookends

PURPOSE

To have students frame their work with good introductory and closing paragraphs.

MATERIALS

- several books used during information gathering (about four or five)
- a set of bookends
- chart of the original research questions
- chart paper
- markers

PRESENTING THE LESSON

Kate begins by showing the students several books they have used during their research. She asks them how many of them used these materials to locate the information they sought. Most of her students raise their hands.

Kate: These were excellent resources during your research because they contain the answers to most of your questions.

Reiko: They were good.

Kate: But look at this.

Kate sets the books on a table and tries to make them stand up alone. No matter how she tries, the books fall over.

Kate: Even though these books were a great resource, they can't seem to stand by themselves. How could we get them to stand?

Luis: How about bookends?

Kate: Great idea! [Pulls out bookends and uses them to hold up the books.]

These books are a lot like your reports. Although they contain excellent facts about the topic, they can't stand alone. They need special supports. The supports you need in your reports are like these bookends. You need something at the beginning and something at the end of your report to allow the facts to make sense to your audience.

You need to write an opening paragraph that gets the attention of your reader and lets the reader know exactly what the report contains. Then, at the end of your report, you need a paragraph to restate all the information that was contained in it. These two paragraphs will act like the bookends did with these books. The bookends gave the support the books needed to allow them to stand on their own. Your opening and closing paragraphs will do the same for your report.

Let's use the big questions we recorded on this chart to compose an opening paragraph that will let readers know what the report will be about.

Kate puts up the chart of big questions on the chalkboard. Next to it she places a large piece of chart paper. She uses a think-aloud strategy to help her students see how it's done.

Kate: Now, to begin with, I need to write a topic sentence that will really make my audience want to read my report. I think it would be good to start off by letting my readers know that I think the whale I wrote about is really interesting. I love beluga whales. Let's see, I think I'd like to start off something like this.

Kate writes the following sentence on the blank chart using a black marker: "Beluga whales are one of the most interesting mammals in the animal kingdom."

Kate: I like that! It lets the reader know that I think beluga whales are special and that they are mammals. Now I need to support this with restatements of the big questions that I intend to answer in my report.

She points to the first big question. She takes a blue marker and writes, "Beluga whales have very distinctive physical characteristics."

Kate: Does this sentence describe my big question?

Marco: Yes. It tells about the physical characteristics of the whale.

Kate: Do you see how I have changed the big question into a statement?

Aileen: That doesn't seem so hard!

Kate now invites students to work in small groups on the other three big questions. Their task is to convert the questions into statements. After a time, Kate asks the groups to share the supporting sentences they came up with. The class decides which supporting sentences are the best, and Kate adds them to her chart. She writes each sentence using the color code that has already been assigned to each big question. When the chart is done, she reads the complete opening paragraph to the class. They think it's great!

Kate: Do you see how I used the big questions to compose a paragraph that will let my audience know what to expect in my report?

Now it's time for you to try. Work in your groups. See if you can write some opening paragraphs that will make your audience want to read the whole report. When you are finished, come show me, and we'll see how you've done.

The students used graphic organizers to write their opening paragraphs. The following is an example of what they came up with.

You can use the same process in another mini-lesson to help students write good endings for their reports. In most cases the endings "tie up" the report by referring to the beginning of the report.

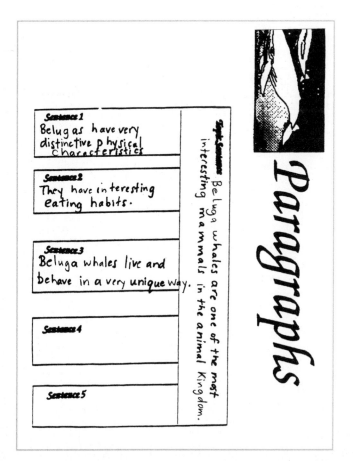
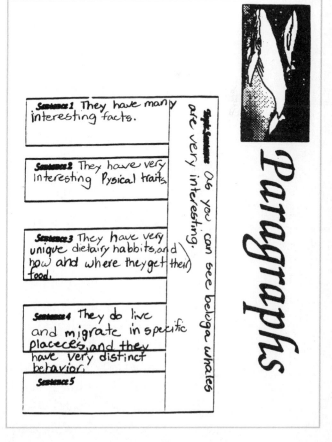

▲ Students use paragraph graphic organizers to plan their opening and closing paragraphs.

Catchy Introductions

Once students see how they can use their big questions to generate a basic introduction, you can then help then make those introductions more engaging. Your students can compare a basic paragraph to one that's a bit more lively and discuss what makes the difference. For example, here's an introduction based on the paragraph organizer on the previous page:

> *Beluga whales are one of the most interesting mammals in the animal kingdom. Beluga whales have very distinctive physical characteristics. They have interesting eating habits. Beluga whales live and behave in a very unique way.*

Your students might contrast that paragraph to one like this:

> *Beluga whales are one of the most interesting mammals in the animal kingdom. In this report, you will learn that beluga whales have very distinctive physical characteristics. You will also find out about their interesting eating habits. Finally, you will learn how beluga whales live and behave.*

Guide students to discuss what was done differently, and what could be done to take the same basic information and make it still *more* interesting. After this discussion students can examine their own introductions and refine them on their graphic organizers.

Kate's students selected these examples as some of their favorite introductions:

- The sperm whale has many unique features, and I'm going to tell you about these features. They are: how they look, what they eat, where they live, and how they behave.
- Here's everything you want to know about killer whales, including their everyday life, their surroundings, and what they eat.
- Shipwrights were very helpful craftsmen. They helped trade grow in colonial America. Did you know that more than half of the ships in England were made in Maryland?
- Hi! I'm one of the first Indians, and I'm going to tell you about Indian food. We eat things like corn. To get it we have to plant it or find it in the wild. We like to cook it in soup.
- The important thing about Native American clothing is that they made it out of animal skins. They wrapped themselves with robes made out of animal skins in the winter.
- The Algonquins wore the most creative things. They painted and tattooed their bodies. They even wore porcupine quills.

The students who wrote these examples discussed specific characteristics that make up good introductions. From their discussion, the class generated a list of characteristics of good introductions:

- catchy first sentence that tells about the topic,
- sentences that tell the readers what they are going to learn,
- using the first-person to pretend you were there,
- interesting facts to grab the reader's attention.

Snappy Endings

Just as a report needs a catchy introduction, it also needs a closing that pulls the report together. Remember, the purpose of the closing paragraph is twofold. First, it should summarize the main points covered in the body of the report. Second, it lets the reader know the report is finished.

Here are some closing paragraphs written by Kate's students:

- Now you should know a lot of interesting things about the bottlenose dolphin. You learned where they live and where they migrate. You learned what their diet is. You learned a lot of physical traits. You learned how they behave. And you learned a lot of interesting facts.
- Isn't the narwhal amazing? Now you know four things about the narwhals—its look, behavior, food, and where it lives. That's the narwhal.
- Now that you have read about the spinner dolphin, don't you agree that they're interesting? Don't you agree that they live all around the world? They dive 60 meters to eat. They have a torpedo-shaped body. The can breech nine and a half feet in the air. That was about the spinner dolphin.
- Now you've learned all about killer whales. You learned about physical traits. You learned about diets. You learned about habitats. You learned about behavior.

You can work with your students to help them end the report with a bang. They can learn to conclude with a final thought that keeps the reader thinking, as illustrated in the following example:

As you have read in this report, the sperm whale has many characteristics that have helped it to adapt and survive for hundreds of years. If people don't interfere, these remarkable creatures will use these characteristics to live on for centuries to come.

Rough Drafts

Once your students have completed their paragraph graphic organizers, they are ready to write their rough drafts. But, as you can see, the main writing task is already done! Students can decide how they want to arrange the paragraphs in their report by sorting the paragraph graphic organizers.

Your students can move from their paragraph graphics to writing their rough drafts.

Revising and Editing

After writing the rough draft, your students will need to revise and edit their work. Revising takes place when students "relook" at their reports to check for meaning and clarity. They first ask themselves whether what they wrote makes sense. They add, delete, change, and rearrange information. Then they ask themselves questions about their work. After they revise their own work by themselves, they meet with a peer editor. We find it helpful to designate corners of the room for this purpose. With this procedure, four pairs of students can meet in the classroom at one time. They take turns asking one another questions such as these:

Revising and Editing Checklist

_____ Does the report seem to tell what is most important?

_____ Is there a good introductory paragraph?

_____ Is there a conclusion?

_____ Does the report have enough information about each subtopic?

_____ Do the ideas flow logically?

_____ Is there a well-ordered sequence without jumping all around?

_____ Does the report include enough details?

_____ Does the report have clear sentences?

Editing occurs when students examine their sentences for clear sentence structure and accurate wording. As you work with your students, you can determine which editing skills they need, and provide mini-lessons to help them. Some skills may be

- rewriting sentence fragments into complete sentences,
- rewriting run-on sentences,
- substituting words and phrases for unnecessarily repeated words and phrases,
- substituting concrete, specific nouns and verbs for more general nouns and verbs,
- using a variety of descriptive words,
- indicating where sections begin and end by starting new paragraphs,
- adding transition words to make the sections fit together,
- using correct spelling, grammar, capitalization, and punctuation.

For example, to support students with transition words, you can have your students brainstorm a list of words that can be good "glue words." Write transition words on a poster for student reference. Here is a list that our students generated:

Time Words: afterward, next, since, then, later, in the end, before, until, finally, earlier, in the beginning, at first, beforehand

Order Words: first, second, to begin with, next, then, finally

Cause Words: because, therefore, as a result, since

You can provide other helpful aids on posters like this one we created with our students:

Tips for Improving Written Reports

1. Proofread for correct grammar, usage, punctuation, capitalization, and spelling.

2. Think about starting a new paragraph when you change topics.

3. Indent each paragraph.

4. Write an interesting title for your report.

5. Write neatly or word process.

In addition, students find that symbols help them to proofread for grammar, capitalization, punctuation, spelling, and words they need to add or delete.

Proofreading Symbols

¶	Begin a new paragraph.	¶ Whales live in the ocean.
∧	Insert omitted word or words.	Whales live in ∧the ocean.
⊙	Insert a period.	Whales live in the ocean ⊙They
Sp	Correct a spelling error.	...in the osean...
≡	Correct a capitalization error.	...in the pacific ocean...
℘	Take out a word.	...in the Pacific pacific ocean...

Making a Bibliography

As an important part of the report-writing process, your students will need to make a bibliography of the sources they used to gather their information. This part can be hard, even for adults. By having your students record the resources they used when they were taking notes (see Chapter 4), you have helped make this task manageable.

Your students can assemble their bibliography from the cards or note-taking sheets they have used during the writing of the report. Using their notes, you can model the development of a bibliography for each type of resource, (e.g., encyclopedia, magazine, multimedia source, trade book). You can post examples for each type of resource in your classroom for easy reference. Below are examples of bibliographies Kate's students have produced.

You can help your students remember the format you want them to use by posting or photocopying a "shell" format like the one on page 94. Note that this shell uses underlining and quotation marks on certain terms to help students remember what to do. You can modify this form to match what you would like your students to do.

Bibliography

Bender, Lionel. Whales and Dolphins. New York: Aladdin Books Ltd, 1988.

Patent, Dorthy Hinshaw. Dolphins and Porpoises. New York: Holiday House, 1987

"Dolphins". World Book Multimedia Encyclopedia, 1996

"Common Dolphin". ACS Cetacean Fact Sheet WWW. acsonline. org

Bibliography

Palmer, Sarah. Killer Whales. Vero beach: Rourk Enterprises, Inc. 1989.

Sattler, Helen Roney. Whales the Nomads of the Sea. New York: Lothrop, Lee & shepard Books, 1987.

"The (Orca) Killer Whale." Discovering Whales http:// whales. magma. com.

"Killer Whales" Cetacean Info at "Whale Song" http:// whales. at. com.

▲ Student bibliographies from the research reports on whales.

Bibliography

Record information about the sources from which you gather information on this form. You can then use it to write your bibliography.

Books

Author _____

Title _____

Publisher _____

Copyright Date _____

Encyclopedia

"Article Title" _____

Encyclopedia Title _____

Volume # _____

Page # _____

Copyright Date _____

CD-ROMs

"Article Title" _____

CD-ROM Title _____

Publisher _____

Copyright Date _____

Magazines

Author _____

"Article Title" _____

Magazine Title _____

Month/Year _____

Page _____

World Wide Web

Item _____

Site: university, museum, organization, etc.
Name of the source of the information or material. _____

Site Address _____

Polishing the Final Report

A s students get ready to present their written reports to a wider audience, it is important to have them take a final look at their work, as published authors do. This is the time to make one last check for a polished product with clear sentences, careful organization, and the conventions of correct spelling, punctuation, grammar, and word usage. That final look may encompass a review of the following aspects:

- **Information**—Do I have enough information to support ideas with clear topic sentences and details?
- **Organization**—Do I have a logical flow of ideas with an ordered sequence?
- **Beginning and End**—Do I have an interesting introduction and a well-developed ending?
- **Clarity**—Do I have clear sentences that make sense to the reader?
- **Finishing Touch**—Do I have a title page and bibliography?
- **Appearance**—Do I have correct punctuation, capital letters, grammar, word usage, and a neat copy?

Kate's students enjoy using *Print Shop Deluxe* (Broderbund, **www.mattelinteractive.com**) to make the title pages for their reports extra special.

The Bottle Nose Dolphin

This report is on the Bottle Nose Dolphin. The Bottle Nose Dolphin has very interesting physical traits. They eat many different. They live in many freshwater rivers and oceans. They behave very oddly and amazingly. They also have amazing facts not in theese catagories.

Bottle Nose Dolphins have very interesting physical traits. They can grow to 10 feet long. They have a beak shaped like a bottle. Bottle Nose Dolphin can swim at speeds up to 25 miles per hour. They have a brain bigger than a humans. They have tail flukes not fins.

The Bottle Nose Dolphin eats many different foods. They eat many different foods. They eat schools of fish or lone fish. Also they eat crabs and shrimp. They eat octopus and squid.

The Bottle Nose Dolphin lives in many places. Some Bottle Nose Dolphins live in freshwater rivers. Sometimes they live on the edge of a continental shelf. They like to stay close to land. Mostly they live near or in the tropics.

One student's research report on the bottle nose dolphin.

Bottle Nose Dolphins behave very oddly. They like to follar fishing boats hoping to get extra fish. They like to ride the waves of ships. They live in family groups of up to 100 dolphins. They vouluntarily go close enough to be touched.

Bottle Nose Dolphins catch their food very amazingly. They catch their food in groups. They use their teeth only to catch their food. They use echo location to find their food. Sometimes they catch fish swimming alone.

Bottle Nose Dolphins also have other interesting facts about them, here are some. They use echo loation to locate their food. They are said to be able to talk to humans. They are the most used dolphin in water shows. They can jump very high out of the water.

That was a report on the Bottle Nose Dolphin. As you can see they have very cool physical characteristics. They have an amazing diet. Their migratory pattern is very interesting. They do behave very odd and amazing.

Beluga Whales

This report is all about beluga whales. You will learn about many interesting facts about them. They have very interesting pysical traits. Their dietary habbits and where and how they get their food is unique. They live and migrate to very specific places, and they have distinct behaver.

There are many interesting facts about beluga whales. The name beluga comes from the Russian word "Belli" meaning white. Belugas are related to Narwhals. Other names for the beluga whale are sea canary, and White whales. Belugas are locally common. Their population is 70,000. Their enemies are polar bears, humans, and killer whales.

Belugas have very interesting pysical traits, and characteristics. Belugas are toothed whales. Belugas can grow up to 18ft. in length, and wiegh up 3,000 pounds. At birth babies are dark brown, or black, and wieghs 175 pounds. Belugas have small round heads and has a short beak. When grown up they have white colored skin.

Belugas have distinct pysical traits. Belugas have two fins on their backs where whales usually have a fin, the beluga has a dorsal ridge instead. In the winter the skin turns yellow because of the cold. Belugas also shed skin continuosly, and my have scratches from polar bears.

Belugas have distinct dietary habits. They eat a veriety of fish, but their favorite is salmon. They also eat lobster, crab, squid, octopus, plankton, mollusk, and shrimp. Belugas are deep bottom divers witch means it dives deep to get its food. Belugas chew and digest their food witch then ends up in a stomach with 4-9 compartments.

A research report on the beluga whale.

Belugas live in cold places. Belugas live in arctic, and sub-artic waters. They live around northern North America, Greenland, Scandinavia, and northern asia. Belugas will migrate up to 620 miles to get to where they are heading. They have been known to travle as far as New Jersey in the United States and to migrate down the Rhin River in Europe.

Belugas behave in many different ways. Belugas live from 25-30 years. Female belugas have only one baby. It takes 14 months till a baby is ready to come out. They travel and feed in groups. There are at least 1,000 in a group. They also make a veriety of moos, clicks, mews, whistles, roars, and grunts.

As you can see the beluga whale is very interesting. They have many interesting facts about them. They have interesting pysical traits. They have distinct pysical traits. They have unique dietary habits, and where and how they get their food. They do live and migrate to specific places, and have distinct behaver.

The End

Technology Tip

Students in Kate's class love to type their final drafts on the computers in the classroom and in the media center. They also like to use the individual desktop word-processor system DreamWriter® (NTS Computer Systems Ltd. **www.dreamwriter.com**), which Kate's school recently purchased. Technology such as this minimizes the chore of writing for students who find handwriting difficult and motivates students in the process.

Students type their final drafts.

We're Almost There!

Now that your students have organized their information into an outline and then into paragraphs, written their rough draft, and revised, edited, and polished their reports, they are ready to present their reports. In Chapter 6 we will discuss options for presenting a final report.

6

Presenting

In this chapter we focus on the final step in the AGOP model—*presenting*. Having your students present their findings in some form is an important part of making the task meaningful. Presenting—whether it is an oral presentation or a display of written reports—gives your students a real audience and acknowledgment of their work.

Oral Presentation or Not?

Not every report needs to be presented orally. But every report should be presented in some way. Together you and your students can decide which reports are better for oral presentations and which are better presented in another way. For example, in Kate's classroom, she and her students decided on the following presentation format for some of the projects they did.

Presentation Format

· Post on bulletin board
· Oral report with diorama to illustrate points
· Written report added to class library (Students give one-minute commercials when they add the report to the collection.)
· Oral report with poster

If you decide not to use an oral presentation for a particular project, your students can still present their work by making it available to others. You should find a place for displaying reports so your students' peers and visitors can enjoy reading them. Kate designates special shelves for class reports. In addition, she often has students' reports on class bulletin boards and in hallway bulletin board displays. Sometimes final projects also are displayed in the media center.

One way your students can present their reports is to post them in the hallway for all to read.

Preparing a Visual Aid for the Presentation

When your students present their reports orally, a visual aid can enhance their presentation and their learning. Posters, paintings, drawings, murals, dioramas, and collages are some examples of the visual displays students like to use. Together you and your students can think about good ways to present the information they have researched. The following mini-lesson shows how students can be included in making this decision. Here we provide guidelines and examples of visual aids your students will enjoy.

MINI-LESSON

How to Show Off Your Knowledge

PURPOSE

To help students determine good formats for presentations.

Kate's class had been reading biographies and autobiographies; this mini-lesson preceded the presentations of their reports on important people. You can use the same approach for whatever topic your students are studying.

MATERIALS

- list of possible formats (or photos or slides of what students have done in the past), including poster or collage, diorama of important event in person's life, vignette of an important event in person's life, time line, photo album of person's home (for example, Clara Barton's home, Monticello, Mount Vernon, etc.), radio or TV interview of the person
- transparency of famous people
- transparency markers

PRESENTING THE LESSON

Kate shows the class the transparency at right listing the names of several famous people.

Presenting Biography/Autobiography

Name	Format
Abraham Lincoln	
Hillary Rodham Clinton	
Frederick Douglass	
Billie Jean King	

Kate: Take a look at the people I have listed on the overhead. I am going to try to decide what would be the best format to choose in depicting the lives of these individuals. Maybe you can help me make a choice. If you have any ideas as I'm trying to decide, please raise your hand.

Kate points to the first name and begins to think aloud.

Kate: Let's see, Abraham Lincoln. He was called the Great Emancipator and was the 16th president of the United States. I know he freed the slaves and was president during the Civil War. I know John Wilkes Booth assassinated him. What would be the best way for me to show something I felt was important in his life? I could visit Ford's Theater in Washington, D.C. It's not far from here. I could visit the museum across the street in the house where he died. Yes, that's what I'll do. And I after I've seen it, I'll make a diorama of either Ford's Theater or the room where he died. That's it! That's what I'll do!

She writes "diorama" on the overhead under Format. She continues to use this think-aloud strategy to complete the chart. She thinks through each person, noting that Hillary Rodham Clinton is the First Lady, running for New York's Senate seat, and that a time line might capture her life well. She does the same for abolitionist/orator Frederick Douglass and for athlete/tennis pro Billie Jean King. Finally, the overhead is complete and looks something like this:

Presenting Biography/Autobiography

Name	Format
◎ **Abraham Lincoln**	diorama of Ford's Theater/room where he died
◎ **Hillary Rodham Clinton**	time line of her life
◎ **Frederick Douglass**	costume and recite quotations
◎ **Billie Jean King**	poster advertising Wimbledon/Bobby Riggs match

Kate: You see, boys and girls, I could have shown something about each of these people in many ways. I tried to think what would be a good way to capture important information about each one. I also tried to think about whether I could complete what I had planned. If I had said I wanted to visit Lincoln's home, I probably wouldn't be able to. It's in Illinois. My plan had to be something I could actually do.

For homework tonight please think about what you would like to do. Think about what you have learned about the famous person you've been reading about. What would make sense for that person? Talk it over with your parents to be sure it's okay. Be prepared tomorrow in class to tell me your idea.

Posters

If students create a poster, they may need your guidelines for writing on large posterboard. A lettering system, such as steno letters or pressed letters, is helpful. Students can trace or press the letters onto the posterboard. In order to center the letters, have students count the number of letters they will have in one line and then start with the middle letter to center the print. Designing the poster includes looking at how the audience will read it from a distance. Students need practice in deciding how to limit the number of words they use and in spacing the words on a specific number of lines.

In Kate's classroom students decided on the criteria they would use to have a "top-notch" poster. They listed them on the board for reference.

Tips for a Top-Notch Poster

- a title that tells what it is all about
- information that is interesting
- just enough words to be clear
- large enough print
- drawings to go with the words
- good spacing between words
- centered lettering

As students presented their reports, they used a table, chair, or peer helpers to hold the posters for all to see. Posters were then placed on a bulletin board as advertisements to persuade students to read their peers' reports, which were displayed either on the bulletin board or on a shelf. Students developed the criteria on page 104 to use in assessing the quality of their posters.

Posters are one way students can present their research.

Name _____ Date _____

Poster Evaluation
(Student Developed)

Element	Points Possible	Points Earned	
		Self	Teacher
1 I included my name and title.	_____	_____	_____
2 The title tells what the poster is about.	_____	_____	_____
3 The picture supports the main idea of the report.	_____	_____	_____
4 All the parts of the poster are correct.	_____	_____	_____
5 The poster is clear with just enough words.	_____	_____	_____
6 There are no errors in mechanics, grammar, or spelling.	_____	_____	_____
7 The poster is neat and presentable.	_____	_____	_____
TOTAL	_____	_____	_____

Did I do my best work? Circle the rating that best describes how you feel about your work.
Then explain why you chose that rating.

Terrific   **Okay**   **Needs Work**

_____

_____

Dioramas

A diorama is another format students may use to enhance their reports. In designing a diorama, students need to think about labeling the parts and creating clear captions. For example, if they create a diorama about how the East Woodland Indians farmed, they need to create captions explaining the steps for growing corn, squash, and beans, and to label parts of the diorama. Students should think about their big questions and key words from their written report to help decide what information to highlight in a diorama.

In presenting the report with a diorama, students choose when to share the diorama during the presentation and how they will describe its contents to the class, especially if the product is not large enough for all to see. For an East Woodland Indians report, students made a sequence chart explaining where the diorama would best fit in their talk. Here is their plan:

1. Tell tribes and languages.

2. Tell how they lived.

3. Explain hunting with weapons and tools.

4. Tell steps they used in planting vegetables (show diorama).

5. Tell how they cooked their food.

6. Tell why Indians lived differently.

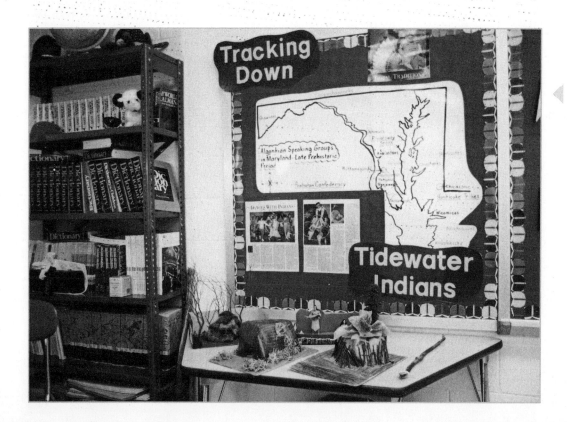

Kate's students used the results of their research on Tidewater Indians to make a diorama of their homes.

Additional Aids to Enhance the Report

n addition to posters and dioramas, your students can create many other aids to enhance their reports. Below is a listing of some popular aids Kate's students use:

audiocassettes	mobiles	cartoons
models	CD-ROMS	multimedia
charts	paintings	collages
photographs	dioramas	posters
drawings	slides	filmstrips
transparencies	maps	videocassettes

Your students can create good old-fashioned "film" strips with scenes on butcher paper that they scroll through cardboard-box "televisions," or they can use software programs to create hi-tech versions. Easy-to-use multimedia programs are available for students. For example, *Kid Pix Studio Deluxe* (Broderbund, **www.mattelinteractive.com**) allows students to create slide shows, complete with sound effects.

Your students can also use audiocassette and videocassette recordings to embellish their reports. For example, students in one class recorded the sounds of whales from a video and used this as part of their oral presentation. For another project, students made and recorded the sounds of Colonial craftsman building a house to use as background "music" while they gave their reports.

Students use a video as part of their presentation. ▷

Maps are also excellent visual aids for some reports. During their whale reports, Kate's students used a special software program, *Mapmaker's Toolkit* (Tom Snyder Productions, **www. tomsnyder.com**), to create maps that showed the migratory patterns of their whales. Others created maps, such as the one below, showing the habitat of their chosen whale.

The media specialist helps a student use special software to create a map of his animal's habitat.

Kate's students make papier mâché replicas of their whales. They tried to make their models accurately reflect the true physical characteristics of the whales they had researched.

The Oral Presentation

Before the talk you will want to give students time to rehearse their report and to work on aspects of public speaking. Students may practice with one another, or they may take time at home to practice giving their report loudly and clearly. Kate's students developed the following guidelines for their peers to use:

Speaking Guidelines

🌀 Speak loud enough for an audience.

🌀 Speak slowly enough.

🌀 Use correct pronunciation and phrasing.

🌀 Know your report well enough that you don't have to read it.

The following mini-lesson is an example of how you can help students improve their oral presentations. Although this approach may be too time-consuming to use for every presentation, occasional use is very valuable to novice presenters.

M I N I - L E S S O N

See for Yourself!

PURPOSE

To have students assess their own areas of need and plan for improvement.

MATERIALS

🌀 speaking guidelines

🌀 video camera

🌀 video tape

🌀 TV with VCR

BEFORE THE LESSON

Kate shares the speaking guidelines with her class. The four guidelines are discussed in order to be sure they are understood by all. Kate demonstrates to her class how each guideline should and should not look, using sample student reports. Kate gives the due date for the oral presentations and explains that the presentations will be videotaped. Each presentation will be taped twice in order to help students make it their best!

PRESENTING THE MINI-LESSON

(This lesson usually takes two or three days to complete.)

Kate: We have discussed the four speaking guidelines for making an oral presentation. Today I am going to videotape your presentations. Afterward I will confer with each of you [this can be done individually or in small groups], and we will use the guidelines to talk about how to improve your presentation.

Kate then videotapes each student's oral presentation. Later she confers with each student. Together they use the guidelines to focus on things the student did well, but they also target areas that could be better. Kate says little during the conferences. She listens as each student assesses his/her performance.

Kate: Now I would like you to choose one thing about your presentation you would like to improve upon. Practice tonight at home. Tomorrow I will tape you again.

The next day she videotapes as students repeat their presentations. At a postpresentation conference, she and the student discuss whether they were able to make the presentation better.

Kate bases the grade for the oral presentation on whether students were able to improve. This technique is a very effective way to have students analyze and refine their speaking skills. They begin to focus on specific ways they can improve, and the goals for better speaking come directly from them.

Back-to-School-Night Tip

You can use the second videotape of the improved presentation as a sample of student work at open house and back-to-school nights! Leave the tape playing in the corner with a note attached indexing the starting numbers for each child's presentation. Parents can rewind or fast forward as necessary to get a glimpse of their child at work.

A "Wax Museum" That Presents a Year of Learning

A group oral presentation that works well is a cumulative activity Kate has her class work on and present at the end of each school year. Over the course of the school year, her class studies about 350 years of Maryland state history. At the end of the school year, Kate's class and the other fourth grades present a "wax museum," with students portraying wax figures that come to life when visitors approach. Students draw on the research they've completed throughout the year to select an important event in Maryland history and write a vignette depicting it. They build sets and make costumes. Parents and other students at the school are invited to tour the museum, which is set up in the auditorium. Tour guides escort the groups through the museum. Students in each scene have memorized a student-composed script introducing each scenario. No student speaks more than two or three minutes. Each student has a part and the parts are well rehearsed. It is a perfect culminating activity and reflects what students have learned during the school year.

Now What?

In this book we have shown you how to take your students through the four steps of the AGOP model: Asking questions, Gathering information, Organizing and writing, and Presenting. In addition, we have shown you how to use your students' reflections to make instruction meaningful at each step along the way. By providing instruction on the unique demands of reading and writing for research, by providing instruction that is meaningful, and by providing lots of opportunities to engage in research, you will help your students become motivated, competent researchers.

Your next stop is your classroom. Try AGOP! You can begin with the ideas we have presented and then build on them to guide your students toward independence and fantastic research reports.

Resources

Bamford, R. & Kristo, J., eds. (1998) *Making facts come alive.* Norwood, MA: Christopher-Gordon.

This useful guide provides annotations of the Orbis Pictus Award winners (an award given annually by the National Council of the Teachers of English for outstanding nonfiction books).

Campbell, J. R. Kapinus, B. A. & Beatty, A. S. (1995). *Interviewing children about their literacy experiences: Data from NAEP's Integrated Reading Performance Record (IRPR) at Grade 4.* Washington, D.C.: National Center for Educational Statistics.

Cunningham, A. E. & Stanovich, K. E. (1991). Tracking the unique effects of print exposure in children: Associations with vocabulary, general knowledge, and spelling. *Journal of Educational Psychology,* 83 (pp. 264–274).

Dreher, M. J., Davis, K. A., Waynant, P., & Clewell, S. F. (1998). Fourth-grade researchers: Helping children develop strategies for finding and using information. *National Reading Conference Yearbook,* 47 (pp. 311–322).

Harvey, S. (1998). *Nonfiction matters.* York, ME: Stenhouse.

Harvey discusses inquiry-based classrooms and the research process; the book includes a section on presenting and assessing student work.

Heiligman, D. (1998). *The New York Public Library kid's guide to research.* New York: Scholastic.

This reader-friendly book is an excellent resource to help your students locate and evaluate resources for their reports. It gives practical advice and easy-to-apply strategies for finding and using materials that are appropriate for a given topic.

Kemper, D., Nathan, R., & Sebranek, P. (2000). *Writers express: A handbook for young writers, thinkers, and learners.* Wilmington, MA: Write Source/Great Source Education Group.

Writers Express is designed for Grades 4 and 5. This book is jam-packed with good advice for your students and will be a great resource for you too.

Leu, D. J., & Leu, D. D. (1999). *Teaching with the Internet: Lessons from the classroom.* Norwood, MA: Christopher-Gordon.

This easy-to-read book is a good source to help you get started on the Internet. It reviews many valuable web sites for students across the content areas, including language arts, and social studies, science.

Levy, P. (2000). *Getting started with the Internet.* New York: Scholastic.

This easy beginner's guide to the Internet tells you everything you need to know to search the Web, ensure Net safety, use e-mail, and much more.

Lewis, M., Wray, D., & Rospigliosi, P. (1994). "…And I want it in your own words." *The Reading Teacher,* 47 (pp. 528–536).

This article offers ideas to help students put the information they locate for reports into their own words. One technique that the authors describe is to use paragraph frames to help students learn common expository text structures.

Marland, M. (1977). *Language Across the Curriculum.* London: Heinemann.

Sebranek, P., Meyer, V., & Kemper, D., (2000). *Write source 2000: A guide to writing, thinking, and learning.* Wilmington, MA: Write Source/Great Source Education Group.

Writers Source 2000 is aimed at Grades 6–8. It is a comprehensive source book that you can use for instruction and your students can consult when they want specific advice.

Strickland, D. S. (1994/1995). Reinventing our literacy programs: Books, basics, balance. *The Reading Teacher,* 48 (pp. 294–302).

Trabasso, T. (1994). The power of the narrative. In Lehr, F. & Osborn J. (Eds.), *Reading, language, and literacy: Instruction for the twenty-first century* (pp. 187–200). Hillsdale, NJ: Erlbaum.

About the Authors

MARIAM JEAN DREHER is a professor at the University of Maryland, College Park, where she teaches reading-education courses. In ten years as an elementary school teacher, she taught fourth grade and sixth grade and served as a Title I specialist. She has published in journals such as *Reading Research Quarterly*, *The Reading Teacher*, and the *Journal of Literacy Research*, and recently coedited the book *Engaging Young Readers: Promoting Achievement and Motivation* (New York: Guilford Press, 2000). Her research interests include helping elementary school students become skilled readers and users of both stories and exposition. She is particularly interested in ways to improve students' ability to engage in research.

KATHRYN A. ("KATE") DAVIS has taught fourth grade at Cashell Elementary in Rockville, Maryland, for the past ten years. Her class has won state recognition for entries in map competitions sponsored by the Maryland Geographical Society and Maryland Historical Society. She was recently nominated for the Disney American Teacher Award. Her background is in special education and elementary education, and she has been teaching in Montgomery County Maryland since 1971. She has presented on AGOP at the International Reading Association Convention, the National Reading Conference, the State of Maryland International Reading Association Convention, the Montgomery County Council of the International Reading Association Conference, and at various schools in Montgomery County. Next year she will be the full-time staff development teacher at South Lake Elementary in Gaithersburg.

PRISCILLA WAYNANT is an instructional specialist working with elementary schools throughout Montgomery County (Maryland) Public Schools. She was a major writer for the county's *Early Literacy Guide* and the *Principal's Guide for Reading/Language Arts Program*. Her past experience includes serving as a classroom teacher, a reading specialist, and a curriculum coordinator. She has taught at all levels, from elementary school through college, and has served as president of the Montgomery County Council of the International Reading Association. Her research interests include expository reading strategies and technology in reading instruction. She regularly presents workshops on improving elementary school instruction at local, state, and national conferences.

SUZANNE F. CLEWELL was coordinator of K–12 Reading/Language Arts in Montgomery County (Maryland) Public Schools and currently consults with school systems. As coordinator she led the development of the *Principal's Guide for the Reading/Language Arts Program* and the *Early Literacy Guide*. She has been editor of the Maryland journal *Literacy Issues and Practices* and served on the editorial advisory board of *The Reading Teacher*. She earned the Maryland award for Distinguished Service from the Maryland Reading Association and the outstanding research award for her work with students' metacognitive behaviors during reading. With her coauthors, she has presented on the AGOP model research at numerous conferences, including the National Reading Conference, the International Reading Association, and the State of Maryland International Reading Association.